A Thinking Man and the Christ

by
Robert K. Hudnut

FORTRESS PRESS
Philadelphia

Library of Congress Catalog Card Number 74–157539

ISBN 0–8006–0100–9

1876C71   Printed in the United States of America   1–100

To Henry Pitney Van Dusen

A Thinking Man Who Knows the Christ

Table of Contents

It is the greatest happiness of the thinking man to fathom what can be fathomed and quietly to reverence what is unfathomable.

Goethe

Preface

This is a book for the average man and his wife who have wondered about their faith. Can they believe in the resurrection? What about the virgin birth? Does the Trinity make sense? How can they teach their children religion?

It is a book for people who want to be as serious about their faith as they are about their jobs. A man will spend fifty weeks a year thinking about how to boost his company's profits. It is the thesis of this book that if he has that kind of intellectual drive he will want to try to boost his faith as well.

Thinking people have much in common. For one thing, a thinking man is honest. He does not claim more than he knows. He knows that he often does not know. He does not presume.

A thinking man is patient. He knows that truth is like mercury from a thermometer. It is devilishly hard to pick up. He keeps trying.

A thinking man is tough. He gets knocked about a bit. Assumptions are one thing. Thinking things through is another. You have to be tough to think things through.

A thinking man is not every man. By no means. Nor is he necessarily loaded with academic degrees. Nor need he be a titan of industry.

A thinking man is any man—or woman—who is restless with assumptions, patient enough to try them, and honest enough to admit that the trial may produce error.

Honest, patient, tough, the thinking man has a lot going for him. When he brings his thinking over into religion, things happen. This book is about what happens.

One thing that happens is that the thinking man changes his thinking. He repents. He does an about-face. But does he change or is he changed?

Another thing that happens is that the thinking man obeys. He submits. Submission does great violence to his normal way of thinking. Nevertheless it happens. The "prince," as Job described himself, becomes, as Paul described himself, the "slave."

A final thing that happens is God. All his life a thinking man has coveted thinking's greatest prize. Ultimately he gets it. Or does it get him? But only for a while. Then it is gone. And the thinking man is once again bending over the mercury on the floor.

A Thinking Man's

Fight for Faith

It is widely assumed that you either believe or you don't. If you do, you're saved; if you don't, you're lost. If you do, you belong to a church; if you don't, you "never darken the door of a church." If you believe, you never doubt; if you doubt, you never believe.

We must avoid such simple answers to such vexing questions. There are no simple answers in religion, just as there are no simple answers in business, or any other field. The gospel may be simple, that "God was in Christ reconciling the world to himself." But believing it is not.

There is in every thinking man a tension between believing and doubting, affirming and denying, hoping and despairing. We may call this tension dialectical idealism. Whatever we call it, the forces of meaning in a thinking man's life are pitted against the forces of meaninglessness. The thinking man struggles to beat chaos into form. How?

I

Step One is aggressive. The thinking man fights. God, the big meaning, is a threat. The thinking man doesn't like to be threatened any more than anyone else, and he rises to a spirited defense.

It is an old story. Jacob wrestled all night with an angel on the banks of the river Jabbok. It was an ancient metaphor for saying that he was defending himself against God. His very name was changed to Israel, which meant, "He who struggles with God."

Moses at the burning bush fought God. "Who am I that I should go to Pharaoh, and bring the sons of Israel out of Egypt?" He was no more captivated by the thought of being captured by God than was Jacob. "They will not believe me. . . . Oh, my Lord, I am not eloquent. . . . Oh, my Lord, send I pray, some other person."

Even the first man and the first woman in the Hebrew myth of creation fought God. God ordered them not to do something, and they did it. "Of man's first disobedience," Milton wrote. The "image of God" is that man can think. "Man is a reed," Pascal wrote, "but he is a thinking reed." And what does man do with his ability to think? He uses it to fight God. It is so natural that the Bible, from the very first story, is saturated with it.

What about us? Is there a thinking man or woman who has not fought God? It is natural for the thinking man to aggress. To think *is* to aggress. "Rebellion" the Hebrews called it. "Pride" the Greeks called it. "Self-reliance" we call it after Emerson. "Atheism" after Nietzsche. "Solipsism" after Ayn Rand, the theory that the self is all.

Now the point is not that these are "bad" words. The point is that they are necessary words to describe the natural condition of a thinking man. To think *is* to aggress. It *is* to fight back. Just as a thinking man will fight to meet the competition in his business, so he will fight to meet the competition in his religion. And his competition, just as it was for Jacob, is God. God wants the thinking man, and the thinking man does not want God.

The first thing to be said, then, about the thinking man, is that he is not neutral. For an unthinking man neutrality is seductive. For the thinking man it is out of the question. *Because* he thinks he can *not* be neutral. "He who is not with me is against me," Christ said. A thinking man is regularly either an atheist or a believer. The one thing he is not is an agnostic. "Don't be an agnostic," Robert Frost said. "Be something!"

II

Step Two is reflective. You cannot aggress forever. You run out of gas. A natural second step in the thinking process is to reflect. Jacob and Moses carried on prodigious deliberations with God. They were not just aggressive, they were reflective.

"The chief question that will be pursued throughout this book," said Dostoevsky about his *The Brothers Karamazov*, possibly the greatest novel ever written, "is the very one from which I have suffered consciously or unconsciously all life long—the existence of God." We fight and then we reflect. Maybe the fight was helpful, maybe not. Maybe it leads us, after reflecting, toward atheism. Maybe it leads toward faith.

Certainly one of the hallmarks of reflection is patience. Patience means not only the ability to endure but the ability to endure pain. And the trouble is that, although fighting back is natural, enduring pain may be less

natural, and we begin to lose our grip on our ability
to think.

> O God, put away justice and truth, for we cannot
> understand them and we do not want them. . . . Leave
> Thy heavens and come down to our earth of waterclocks
> and hedges. Become our uncle. Look after Baby, amuse
> Grandfather, . . . help Willie with his home-work,
> introduce Muriel to a handsome naval officer.
> Be interesting and weak like us, and we will love you
> as we love ourselves.[1]

Certainly another mark of reflection is openness.
We are open at all times to the possibility of God.
We are ready to be surprised by God. It is like the
wind, Christ said to Nicodemus. "You do not know
whence it comes or whither it goes." It is unpredictable.
But we must be ready for it. We must position
ourselves to feel it. "Chance," said Pasteur, "favors
the prepared mind."

Things, then, can happen in our openness. We can be
pulled either toward atheism or belief. Which will it be?
We cannot answer in the abstract. We have to think
back—that is, reflect—on what has happened to us the
past week and month and years. We have to reflect on
the moments which, in our openness and patience,
drew us toward faith or unbelief.

That is what we do when we pray. To pray is to
reflect on what has happened to us to see if there is any
possibility of God in it. "Surely the Lord is in this place,"
Jacob said once when he was reflecting, "and I did not
know it." "Sometimes," says Blanche in the arms of her

---

[1] W. H. Auden, "For the Time Being, A Christmas Oratorio,"
© 1945 by W. H. Auden in *The Collected Poetry of W. H. Auden*
(New York: Random House, 1945), p. 457. Reprinted by per-
mission.

lover in Tennessee Williams's *A Streetcar Named Desire,*
"there is God—so quickly."

III

Step Three is submissive. It is the hardest step a
thinking man has to take. We aggress. We reflect.
We submit. The first is natural, the second less natural,
the third unnatural.

It is one thing to fight, another to endure, but quite
another to give up. It is the last thing in the world a
thinking man wants to do. Because he is so stunned with
his ability to think, to be not just a reed but a thinking
reed, he resists giving up down to the last battlement.

The natural thing is to go all the way with the fight
and become an atheist. The natural thing is to adulate
the self at the expense of everything that threatens the
self—be it God or state or family or whatever.

The unnatural thing is to think oneself into submission.

> God has put me in the wrong [Job cried],
>   and closed his net about me.
> Behold, I cry out. "Violence!" but
>   I am not answered;
> I call aloud, but there is no justice.
> He has walled up my way so that
>   I cannot pass,
>   and he has set darkness upon my paths.
> He has stripped from me my glory,
>   and taken the crown from my head.

We aggress. We reflect even. But we do not submit.
We fight. We endure. But we do not give up. It is
unnatural. It is an affront to our humanness.
It is *impossible.*

The word is not original, it is Christ's. "Who *can* be
saved?" his disciples asked. "With men," Jesus said,

"it is impossible, but not with God; for all things are possible with God."

Faith is a thinking man's fight to submit. Why does he do it? Why does he go through with it? Why does he position himself to the point where God can take over rather than position himself, which is the natural thing, to the point where he can take over God?

The only answer seems to be that the thinking man realizes that it is his uniqueness as a thinking man to think the thought that he would not naturally think. "The idea of God," Calvin said, "is naturally engraved on the hearts of men." But that was four hundred years ago. It is not the same now. The thinking man now is increasingly void of the God-thought. It is increasingly difficult for him to think it. Why? Because *he* is increasingly God.

Knowledge is doubling every ten years, according to the National Education Association.[2] Industrial production, according to the Babson Institute, is doubling every sixteen years.[3] This means, among other things, says the *New York Times,* that there will have been as much growth in our economy between 1965 and '85 as between the Pilgrims' time and 1965.[4] When man is God, the God-thought is alien to man-thinking.

It is only a matter of degree, of course. Clearly men in biblical times thought they were as godlike as we. That is why the Bible is a history of rebellion. It is also why Jesus was forever backing the thinking men of his day to the wall. He was continually telling them to do

[2] *Time,* 26 January 1965.
[3] *Newsletter,* 12 July 1965.
[4] *New York Times,* 7 November 1965.

things he knew they could not possibly do. "Sell what you have and give to the poor." He knew the rich man could not do it. "Love your enemies." He knew they could not do it. "Be ye therefore perfect." He knew it was *impossible*. He issued these radical demands to throw the thinking men of his day onto the radical mercy of God. "With men it is impossible." That is *precisely* the point he was trying to make. "But not with God; for *all* things are possible with God."

IV

Step Four therefore is grace. Faith is the fight to submit. It is going from aggressive to reflective to submissive thinking. Then grace takes over because, try as we will, we cannot finally submit. It is too unnatural.

Two things are obvious. One, that the fight for faith is necessary. There is no peace without war; there is no heaven without hell. We must aggress, we must reflect, we must try to submit. If we do not, it is entirely possible that grace will *not* strike. We must *position* ourselves so that grace *can* strike. A man who does not *fight* God may not be in *position* to receive God's grace. That is the point of the Jacob story and the Moses story and the Job story and the Jesus story and the Paul story. Paul was on his way to arrest a group of Christians when God's grace struck. Jesus did not get going in his ministry until he had been bewildered in the wilderness.

Nor is a man who does not reflect in position for grace to strike. We must not limit grace, of course. It is such that it *can* strike anywhere. "The wind blows where it will," Jesus said. But he said it to an enemy,

Nicodemus, who had *come* to Jesus to *reflect* with Jesus on how a man *could* be born again.

Nor is a man who does not at least *try* to submit to God in a good position for grace. Jesus said to his disciples "with men it is impossible" after the rich man had turned away from them sorrowing because he would not sell what he had and give to the poor. He did not even *try* to submit. The disciples, who walked with Jesus for three years, did everything in their ability as thinking men to submit. The results are apparent. We never hear of the rich man again. But we are Christians today because of the disciples.

The other obvious thing, then, to be said about grace is that it is powerful. It took Paul, for instance, a man who had held the coats of a mob while they threw rocks at a man's head, and turned him from a murder-accomplice into a saint.

Grace took Job, a well-to-do businessman mesmerized by his ability to think and to fight God with his marvelous thinking machine, and turned him into a man who could be used by God.

Grace took Moses, a murderer, and turned him from a fugitive into one of the greatest leaders in the history of the world.

Grace took Jesus, and kept him in its grip all the way to the end, where it gave us the most stunning example history has ever seen of power, whether you call it fact or metaphor, the resurrection.

V

Step Five: grace can take us. How? It can change our thinking. That is what the word "repent" literally means.

It is an important word for the thinking man. Now we no longer think of ourselves as thinking men but as children. Again, the word is not original, it is Christ's. "Children," he called his disciples. It was the right metaphor for submissive thinking. "Whoever does not receive the kingdom of God like a child. . . ."

Paul took the metaphor a step further. He called himself a "slave." A slave does not think for himself. A slave submits. "We take every thought," he wrote, "captive to obey Christ." "To me to live *is* Christ."

Christ himself, of course, lived the metaphor best. He was the suffering servant. He had so submitted his thinking to God, that he would serve him even to the point of suffering.

And that is the other way grace takes hold of us. Its power is such that it empowers us to be suffering servants, too. Our power is our obedience. It is our slavery. It is our willingness to obey God. It is our alacrity in accepting Christ's orders.

The thinking man not only thinks, he acts. He not only submits, he serves. Without the service, the thought is academic. Without the suffering if need be, the thinking is quixotic. In the old language: faith prepares us for grace, and grace produces works.

Grace, in Bonhoeffer's memorable word, is not cheap. As we have discovered, it comes, usually, only after a fight. And now it remains, usually, only after another kind of fight. The first fight was in a man's mind; the second is in his heart. The first was in his thinking; the second is in his acting. The first involved only himself in his aloneness; the second involves other people in his togetherness.

Jesus told the thinking men of his day that the grace in which they stood was no good if it did not result in doing good. It was unthinking if it did not involve acting. It was not the love of God if it did not mean the love of man. "Let your light so shine before men that they may see your good works. . . ." "If you do not forgive men their trespasses, neither will your Father forgive your trespasses."

Grace is not cheap. It is a fight to get, and it is a fight to keep. But when the orders come they are obeyed. "Go," Christ commanded, "and do likewise." At the side of the road, in the home, the school, the job, the community, the nation, the world. Do what? Respond, in love to the uttermost, to the agony of the world. "I was hungry and you gave me food, I was a stranger and you welcomed me, I was sick and you visited me." If we are not doing those things in our jobs and our homes and our communities and our world, then the grace in which we allegedly stand is cheap. More to the point, it is worthless.

If, however, a thinking man does all in his power to bind up the wounds of the world, beginning with Joe's wound at the coffee break, then he will have begun to beat chaos into form and meaninglessness into meaning. The fight for faith will have turned into the love of man. What more could anyone ask?

Can a Thinking Man

Be a Christian?

"The scholar," Emerson observed, "is man thinking."
But his definition was too tight. Most scholars are
thinkers, to be sure, but not all thinkers are scholars.
By man thinking we do not mean a genius. We do not
mean a scholar. We mean anyone who uses his head
and is able to cope, reasonably well, with life.
Shepherds as well as wise men came to the Christ.

The Christian is one who thinks certain thoughts.
To be sure, Christians *do* certain things and *feel* certain
things and maybe even *are* certain things. But, for
now, we are interested in what Christians *think*.
A Christian, by definition, is one who thinks that Jesus
was the Christ. That is, he looks upon the ancient
Jewish expectation of a Messiah, God's anointed, as
having been fulfilled in this man. And fulfilled in a
unique way: "God shows his love for us," a Christian
once wrote, "in that while we were yet sinners Christ
died for us." Or, as another Christian once put it:
"For God so loved the world that he gave his only
begotten son."

Being a Christian, then, means thinking these thoughts:
(1) that there is a God; (2) that he is most fully
revealed in Christ; (3) that the key to the mystery of
life is somehow in that man's and that God's
suffering love.

The question is, Can a thinking man think these thoughts without violating his integrity?

I

There are those who say he cannot. For one thing, their argument goes, the more we know the less necessary God is. The more a thinking man knows the more he is able to cope with life's problems and the less he needs someone or something to help him cope. God was necessary in Christ's day when people were untutored and scientific knowledge nil. Particularly he was needed by the Christians who were the most untutored. He was needed as a reservoir of answers into which to toss life's question marks. He was needed as a cosmic crutch on which to lean as they hobbled through the universe.

But now, God is not needed. We know so much more. We don't need God to explain a thunderstorm or a defeat or a victory or a disease. We know all these things. We have all these answers. And where we don't have them we're working on them. We're working on Vietnam and cancer and water pollution.

For another thing, believing in God is an admission of dependence as well as of ignorance. The rhythm of life from childhood through adolescence and on toward maturity is to become independent, to stand on your own feet. Many of our psychiatric problems can be traced to excessive dependence. But the more a person knows the less dependent he will be. Only the weak believe in God. Only the ignorant believe in God.

The argument is stock and the answer, I suppose, equally stock. The fact of the matter is that we don't know as much as we think we know. We may be in the process of conquering outer space, but we are no farther along in conquering inner space than we were in Christ's day. As a matter of fact, a good case could be made for our being *less* far along. In those days every man, woman and child on the face of the planet did not go to bed with fifteen tons of TNT strapped to his back.

Furthermore, it may be argued, the more we know the *more* necessary God is, the more we need someone or something to stand in the way of our basking in the sunshine of our own achievements. Perhaps only God is big enough to do that. There is a diabolism in us that impels us to self-congratulation when, because of our brains, we achieve. It is hard for a $15,000-a-year man to be a Christian. Doubly hard for a $30,000—; triply hard for a $45,000—.

Augustine put it succinctly in his comments on the demise of Rome. Rome, he said, was felled by "self-love in contempt of God." Reinhold Niebuhr put it equally well back in 1939 when the most intelligent nation in the world's history was basking in the sunshine of its own achievements:

> [The temptation to trust self rather than God] is particularly great when [our] achievements are especially imposing. . . . Hence periods of prosperity inevitably lead to the corruption of the Christian faith, while periods of adversity prompt men to probe more deeply into the nature and meaning of human life.[1]

II

Another argument against a thinking man's being a Christian is that as a non-Christian he can do the things

[1] Reinhold Niebuhr, *Beyond Tragedy* (New York: Scribner's, 1955), p. 114.

a Christian does without having to think the things a
Christian thinks. This is the argument of the happy
humanist who says, in effect: "I can love without
Christ; I can be good without God; I can obey the
Golden Rule without having to figure out the theology
that goes with it. What more could you ask?"

Precisely. You can ask a great deal more. The ethic
doesn't go nearly far enough without its theology.
As a happy and brilliant humanist once said to me:
"I don't kill you because I don't want your friends to
kill me." But that isn't enough. Enlightened self-interest
isn't enough. Even humanitarian humanism does not
go far enough.

Calcutta, India, Associated Press, April 13, 1966:

> The sign over the door reads "Home for Dying Destitutes."
>
> Inside, 66 men and 72 women lie on steel frame cots
> waiting for the end to come.
>
> These people are products of this population-choked
> city, which hardly has time to care for the living.
>
> Some of the men and women here were forced to leave
> hospital beds when they were termed incurable, to
> make room for those who might be saved.
>
> Others were among the countless thousands of nameless
> persons whose homes are Calcutta's sidewalks and
> gutters. Work is scarce and begging is fruitless.
>
> People like these used to die anonymously. In the
> old days, trucks picked them up and dumped them
> into the Hooghly River, an arm of the Ganges.
>
> Then in 1952, Mother Teresa, Superior General of the
> Roman Catholic Church's "Missionaries of Charity,"
> took over a former temple rest house for Hindu pilgrims
> and made it a haven for the dying. Since then, 18,000
> persons have gone to the crowded stucco building on a
> cluttered street in Calcutta. Of these, 8,500 died. But,

amazingly, the others, most of whom have to be carried
into the home, regained strength and the will to live
and walked back out into the city streets.

How many humanist homes for dying destitutes are
there in India? How many hospitals? How many
orphanages? How many leprosy clinics?

It's a nice ethic, a fine ethic. But without the theology
it often does not go far enough. The dynamic, the
power, often are not there.

Twenty men visit weekly in a jail. They are neither
lawyers nor social workers. They are thinking men with
God somewhere behind them. There are *no* other
non-God-backed thinking men visiting in that jail.

III

Another argument against a thinking man's being a
Christian is that he will not be a hypocrite. Much as
he might like to believe the three—God, Christ, suffering
love—and so have a more dynamic ethic, he will not
compromise his intelligence to get them. He will not
lie for God. He will not be dishonest. He will not
pretend to be something he is not. God, the argument
goes, does not want any more phonies than he
already has.

It's a good argument. No one likes a hypocrite. But
the argument is not convincing. For one thing, no one
is being asked to be a hypocrite. Christianity asks
no one to say he believes something when he doesn't.
Better an honest atheist than a phony Christian any day.

For another thing, the argument has an implicit
assumption which is at best naive and at worst

dangerous. When a person says that he will not be
a hypocrite, he is obviously implying that to think
what a Christian thinks is to do violence to the way he
thinks as a thinking man. But is such violence done?

The thinking man thinks in many ways. Only
unthinking men limit themselves to one. There is, for
instance, the two-plus-two way, which is admirably
suited for certain results. There is also the
"How-do-I-love-thee? Let-me-count-the-ways" type of
thinking, which is equally well suited for other results.
Whenever the two ways are confused the results
are irrelevant.

> When a fellow kisses a girl [a doctor explained on a
> radio program] the adrenosympathetic system calls on
> the liver for glycogen for energy. This in turn forces
> the release of insulin, vitamin B–1, and phosphorus
> to burn the sugar. . . . There is an exchange of starch,
> phosphorus, and thiamine between the thalamic
> and the cortical brain. . . .

There is, of course, something more going on in a kiss
than that. And there is, of course, far more going on in
the world than one way of thinking would permit
us to discover.

Thus we arrive again at one of the chief characteristics
of the thinking man: openness to truth. When we say
that the thinking man is open to truth we are not so
much defining what that truth is as we are defining an
attitude toward any truth. It is important to begin with
attitudes rather than answers. An answer, no matter how
cogent, is powerless before the wrong attitude. This is
why businessmen clinch many important contracts over
lunch. They want to create the right attitude. There is
even occasional liquid inducement toward creating
the right attitude.

The attitude of the thinking man, as opposed to the unthinking man, is the right one from the start. He is open to truth, no matter where the truth may come from. A thinking Republican will be fully aware of the need for social responsibility. A thinking Democrat will be equally aware of the need for individual initiative. Both will be open to the truth about black ghettoes.

Similarly the Christian will be open to truth from the secularist. For many people God *is* dead, and his death is a judgment on Christians who have not brought him to life. For many people Christ was a great man and that's it, and their insistence on his radical humanness should be remembered by Christians. For many people the church *is* irrelevant, and churchmen should realize that it is time, in the current cliché, to let the world write the agenda.

By the same token, the secularist, the cynic, the agnostic, the atheist, if he is a thinking man, will be open to truth from the Christian. He will realize that there is a dimension to life that he is missing, and that life may be too short to miss that much. Far from asking him to be hypocritical in coming over into that dimension, the Christian is asking him to use his thinking powers to the full and thus *inevitably* come over into that dimension.

You can call it the dimension of height, or you can call it the dimension of depth. You can call it the dimension of transcendence, or you can call it the dimension of mystery. The metaphor is not important. The experience is. Every thinking man is, *by definition,* involved in this experience.

It is impossible for the thinking man not to ask questions. The first thinking experience in Jesus' life of which we have any record is of his being in the temple and asking questions. You cannot ask questions and not some day arrive in the dimension of depth. A thinking man asks the question about his own dying. He asks, Why does she love me? He asks, as he looks in on his children at night, What did I do to deserve them?

All the thinking man has to do is be himself and he will be in the right attitude for becoming a Christian. "Ask," Christ said, "and it will be given to you."

A final answer to the hypocrisy argument is the one which reminds us that the other leading characteristic of the thinking man is his honesty. A thinking man, by definition, cannot be a hypocrite. It is a contradiction in terms. If the thinking man will only be himself, he cannot help being open and honest.

The temptation to play a role, however, which is where the word "hypocrisy" comes from in the Greek, to pretend, to lie for God is real. It is there for everyone who ever joins a church. Why?

Because the thinking man, who is honest, knows that he does not always know. He knows, strangely, that the more he knows the more he knows he does not know. The more he asks, the more he is open to truth, the more he seeks to bring the light of his thinking to bear on the dark corners of human thought, the more he knows he may not succeed. The temptation to close the door is real.

If we are honest, we will admit that we do not always approach the dimension of mystery with hope. Often it makes us shudder. Often it arouses what has been called "holy dread." Often it creates what the Jews

called "fear of the Lord." And because we are
afraid, we draw back.

But if we are honest, we will also admit that there is
something in us, because we are *thinking* reeds, that
draws us irresistibly forward. It may be a siren, as in the
old Greek myth, luring us to our own destruction. It may
be a serpent, as in the old Hebrew story, enticing us to
adventure beyond the limits of human knowledge.
Or it may be God, as in the old Christian history, offering
us the promise of new life in an old Christ.

A thinking man is open to the possibility that it is God,
as the thinking man was who brought his epileptic son
to Christ. He was open to the power of suffering love.
And he was honest. "I believe," he said. "Help
my unbelief!"

A Thinking Man's

Obedience

A thinking man is alarmed when his thinking is
threatened. It is threatened whenever he is asked to obey.
He is asked to obey the state, the boss, the god,
sometimes even the wife. But his mind is the thinking
man's most prized possession, and he yields it only
with reluctance.

He knows, of course, that he must yield. It is foolish
to quarrel with traffic laws and with the usual rules of the
game at the job and at home. But when it comes to
yielding to God, that is a different matter. Very different.
A thinking man, as we have seen, yields to his god
only with a fight.

Now to be sure, there are some gods to which it is easy
to yield. The job itself can become a thinking man's god
and he can pledge his ultimate allegiance to it. Or a
thinking man's family. Or his state. We are Americans
with really very little difficulty. Very few of us have ever
considered being anything else.

But when it comes to yielding ourselves to God, we
balk. What should, perhaps, be the ultimate allegiance
becomes, for the thinking man, the ultimate debate.
He was born an American and he was born, say, a
Christian, but, where the birthright of the first is

accepted, the birthright of the second must, it seems, be rejected before it can be accepted.

This is why the thinking man is, by definition, fascinated by religion. He knows that it is the realm of transcendent loyalty—loyalty greater even than that to job, home, country. He knows that obedience to God can even put him into conflict with obedience to America. Religion is therefore the most alluring area of his thought-life. He tackles it with gusto and agony. He is alternately attracted and repelled.

I

The way Jesus was. His ability to think must have been staggering. He was drawn into a wilderness of doubt, into the aloneness of death, and yet his allegiance, his loyalty, his obedience was such that nearly a billion people now look on him as the thinking man who most completely allowed his thinking to be dominated by his God.

Certainly there were others who were obedient. Maybe if Moses had also been executed, he would have been thought as obedient. But we know too much of Moses' background. He killed a man. Maybe David, but he too had had a man killed in order to get the man's wife. Maybe Abraham, but he was too shrouded in mystery. Maybe Isaiah or Jeremiah, but they were never quite heroes enough.

Only this man was so obedient that his fellow thinking men called him by the name above all names that speaks obedience. They called him "slave." He was God's slave. Whatever God commanded him he would do, even die. Whatever God told him to speak he would speak, even "treason," even "blasphemy." Wherever

God commanded him to go he would go, even to lepers.

To "hear" in the Hebrew meant to "obey." To hear God's word meant to obey it. It was a religion of the word because it was a religion of action. And it was a religion of the word because thinking men used words to think their thoughts. It was not at all surprising, then, that the one man, the slave, was also called "the word."

II

But what about the other men? What about the men like us who had their flaws? They were disobedient. Not all of them all of the time, to be sure, but enough of them enough of the time to have it reported.

In the very first story a thinking man and woman could not stand not knowing, any more than we can. They wanted to think more than they wanted to obey. "Don't eat," God said. Those were their orders. But they did not want to obey, they wanted to think. They wanted to eat of the fruit of the tree of *knowledge*. Precisely because they could think, they did *not* want to obey. They had to reject before they could accept, disobey before they could obey, be repelled before they could be attracted, use their brains before, with their brains, they would consent to be slaves.

The only difficulty with this approach was that it didn't work, and when they lost their God they lost their country, too, and their jobs and their home. They were thrown out, exiled, condemned to wander because they had not obeyed.

Now let's not make the mistake of thinking this is just a story. Obviously it is, but it wouldn't have lasted three thousand years if it were not *our* story, too, the

story of men, the history, if you will, of man thinking.
We are bewitched by our ability to think. We are
enthralled with the fact that our thinking puts us, above
all the animals, in the image of God. And because we
are so enraptured with ourselves and our ability to
think, we have no time for obedience. Who wants to be
a slave when, because of his brain, he can be free?
Who wants to obey when, because he is a thinking man,
he can think for himself?

III

Christ was obedient. He was a slave. We are
disobedient. We are thinking men. But Christ was a
thinking man, too. Therefore, we, too, could be obedient.
What does it take? Why should we even attempt it?
For the following reasons:

One, obedience means freedom. It is one of the
Christian paradoxes. But it works. "He who would save
his life will lose it. He who loses his life for my sake
will find it." He who is bound to Christ, in other words,
comes into his own as a free man.

Paul was forever referring to his fellow Christians
as slaves of Christ. Why? Because he and they knew that
in that slavery they had at last found freedom. "We . . .
take every thought," Paul the thinking man said,
"*captive* to *obey* Christ." Why? Because, as he put it,
"For freedom Christ has set us free."

Now on the face of it this may seem difficult to
understand, even for thinking men. But consider.
When a man becomes bound to his job, "wrapped up,"
as we say, in his work, he is on the one hand no longer
enslaved to job insecurity, and he is on the other hand

freed to be creative. Every man knows that the more he is bound to his job the freer he feels, and that when he is jobless he is enslaved to all sorts of self-doubt, domestic quarrels, and so on.

The point is that we take on progressively more binding attachments in life in order to become progressively freer. The Christian position is a paradox, all right, but it is a paradox that works.

Two, obedience means faith. Faith *is* obedience. Faith is *doing* what Christ *commands* the thinking man to do.

There are perhaps few finer examples of mid-century thinking men than that of Dietrich Bonhoeffer. He was on his way to becoming one of the world's leading theologians when he left the safety of New York and went back to his native Germany to stand by his people under the Nazis. Ultimately he was executed in a prison camp. But before he died he wrote something which could well be the hallmark for all thinking men who are fascinated by the outrageous demands of Christ:

> Unless he obeys a man cannot believe. The step of obedience must be taken *before* faith can be possible. . . . If you dismiss the word of God's *command,* you will not receive his word of grace. . . . The gracious call of Jesus now becomes a stern command: Do this! Give up that! Leave the ship and come to me! . . . Jesus says, *"First obey,* perform the external work. . . ." If you *don't* believe, take the first step all the same, for you are bidden to take it. No one wants to know about your faith or unbelief. Your *orders* are to perform the act of obedience on the spot. *Then* you will find yourself in the situation where faith becomes possible. . . .[1]

[1] Dietrich Bonhoeffer, *The Cost of Discipleship* (New York: Macmillan, 1963), p. 72 (ital. added).

We have waited around to be struck by some
heavenly vision when we should have gotten out there
and done what God's words were telling us to do. It is
most interesting that the Jews never knew anything
about visions of God. All they knew were auditions.
They had to be able to *hear* him, hear his incredible
words, and then *do* what those words *commanded* them
to do. To hear *meant* to obey.

If, then, we would believe—and it is entirely possible,
as thinking men, that we will choose not to—if we would
believe, it is essential to *position* ourselves so we can
hear. How do we do that? We obey. What do we obey?

Three, obedience means other people. We obey
Christ's *orders* to love other people. What does "love"
mean? It has long since become a cliché, like "faith." Love
means something specific. Christ never left you hanging.
He was always specific. That was what got him
into trouble.

Your *orders*, he said, are to feed the hungry, welcome
the stranger, clothe the naked, visit the sick, go to those
in prison. Five things, among others. When did we
last do them?

Don't talk about whether or not you believe in God.
Go to a jail and *earn* the right to talk. Position
yourself to the point where your talk will make sense,
where it will be a thinking man's talk. Nobody has any
business talking about God on the coffee break or in
the dormitory or, for that matter, in the church until
he has *first* positioned himself to hear God talking to him
by doing something for his North Vietnamese neighbor,
his Detroit neighbor, his Watts neighbor,
his AFDC neighbor.

Four, obedience therefore means danger and even death. Christ never minimized his terms. He never cut the cost of discipleship. "Follow me" was not a Greek vision. It was two *words* that, if you heard them and *therefore obeyed* them, could cost you your life.

> Five times I have received at the hands of the Jews the forty lashes less one. Three times I have been beaten with rods; once I was stoned. Three times I have been shipwrecked; a night and a day I have been adrift at sea.

A thinking man likes risk. Danger attracts him. He is even willing to suffer for what he believes—that is, for the way he obeys. "I will show him how much he *must* suffer," Christ said at the conversion of Paul, "for the sake of my name."

Five, obedience means hard mental as well as physical work. As we have seen, it demands a violent wrench in the thought processes. Christ demanded that wrench, one commentator has put it, with "pitiless severity."[2] "Repent," he said, "and believe in the gospel." The Kingdom of God, Christ said, is entered "violently."

Once again the action is first, the belief second; the work first, the faith last. "Repent." It meant change your thoughts. "We . . . take every thought captive to obey Christ." The "thought" that was to be enslaved is the same root as the word "repent." To repent *meant* to enslave your thoughts. It was hard enough to enslave your actions and to prove your slavery in your love. It was equally hard to enslave your thoughts and to prove your slavery in your changed thinking. Nevertheless, this was another action that was required. Not requested, note, but required; not asked, but commanded.

[2] J. Behm in *Theological Dictionary of the New Testament*, ed. G. Kittel, vol. 4 (Grand Rapids: Eerdmans, 1967), p. 1003.

"God's definitive revelation [in Christ]," writes the commentator on this violent word, "repent," "demands final and unconditional decision on man's part . . . a transformation of nature, . . . a resolute turning to God in total obedience."[3] It is an order.

Six, why be a slave? Because slavery means God. It is the only way. You can be the servant of your friends. You can serve in your job. You can serve in your home. You can serve your community and your country. But to know God a thinking man must be his slave. Being his servant is not enough. The word Paul used was "slave." Why? Because a thinking man's god is, by definition, his *ultimate* allegiance.

But it is not, fortunately, just a matter of our getting to know God. It is a matter of God's getting to know us. If a thinking man can think his way through to his slavery, he will be astounded to discover that he is not— nor was he ever—alone. God was with him.

We cannot finally love. We cannot finally believe. We cannot finally repent. Which is to say we cannot finally obey. Because we are thinking men and made in the image of God, we cannot finally be slaves. It did not work in the myth of the first man, and it does not work for us. The wrench is too violent. The work is too hard. The freedom on the other side of slavery is never alluring enough. We need help.

"God," said the poet Edwin Arlington Robinson, "is the name that comes to me when I think and feel how little I have to do with what I am." God is the name that comes to us when we find ourselves the slaves of Christ. It was too much to do on our own.

---

[3] Ibid., p. 1002 (ital. added).

A Thinking Man's

Position

What is helpful about Christianity is its ability to set priorities. Out of the welter of conflicting demands upon a thinking man, Christianity is able to slice through to what is most important. Its contribution to psychic and social stability is, therefore, incalculable.

No longer need a thinking man be at sea about ultimate values. No longer need he be uncertain about ultimate meaning. No longer need he cast about for the way he should be running his life. Now he knows, because Christianity has told him, that this is first, this second, this third.

He may not, of course, care for these priorities. They may do violence to his normal way of doing things. They may appear to him to be upside down, and he may not want to live in what is, ostensibly, a topsy-turvy world. Nevertheless, if he would be a Christian, his priority order is set, it is written in cement, and, far from upsetting his world, Christianity tells him that his world is, for the first time, perhaps, right side up.

I

God first. "You shall love the Lord your God," Jesus said, "with all your heart, and with all your soul, and with all your mind. This is the great and *first* commandment."

Now Jesus is not, of course, the one who gave the commandment. He is simply quoting the Hebrew Scriptures. Nor was he the first to lift the commandment out as number one. The Jews knew perfectly well that it was the most important. What was unique about Jesus was his ability, again and again, to slice through to the heart of the matter and to remind his fellow Jews of their priorities.

The ancient Jews, as we know, had a penchant for nit-picking, for seeing the trees and missing the forest, for getting bogged down in the details of their law and forgetting its origin. And, in this respect, I doubt that they were much different from many, if not most, of us. We, too, get so wrapped up in the trivial that we miss the eternal. We get so enamored of little meanings that we forget the big ones. We get so caught up in lesser values that we neglect ultimate values. "God first" is difficult for thinking men to accept.

To put God first, we respectfully suggest, is outmoded. It may have been the normal thing to say or even to try to do in Jesus' time, but it is most certainly not the normal thing in our time. The normal thing is to put self first, or job first, or family first, or nation first. The last thing in the world most of us would think of doing is putting God first.

Why is God first? Maybe if we knew why, that would make him first for us. Certainly there are many reasons for a thinking man to put God first, but let's try these.

There is what we might call the *psychological* reason. A thinking man puts God first because it gives him a fuller life. Without God first the divine dimension to life is either lost or relegated so far into the background that it is rarely found. "I came that you may have life," Christ said, "and have it more abundantly." Life is fuller the more we try to put God into it, and, if we are going to have God in it at all, he has to be first. A god is, by definition, what comes first in a person's life.

There is also what we might call the *sociological* reason for putting God first. A thinking man does so because it helps him lead a better life. The argument is not just fuller but better living. With God we are, or at least we can be, better people than without. People who have God behind them can get very worked up about social injustice and tyranny and starvation and people in jails and hospitals and nursing homes. "I was hungry," Christ said, "and you gave me food, I was sick and you visited me."

There is also what we might call the *theological* reason for putting God first. A thinking man does so because he is commanded to. "This is the great and first *commandment*." It is not a suggestion. It is not a request. It is not simply a teaching. It is God's command. The greatest virtue of the thinking man is not faith but obedience.

Now we may not like this. It may be an affront to our dignity. It may be too Teutonic for our American blood. Germans are great ones for following orders, which, as may be recalled, was Eichmann's sole defense. Americans are equally great for freedom, self-reliance, and not being ordered around by anyone.

But here God is ordering, and God is saying that he shall be put first in a man's life. It is the great commandment, Jesus explains. It is the first commandment. And it is a *commandment*. The Christian —or Jew, for that matter—is under orders to obey it.

So often it seems that the commands have evaporated from modern life. The commanding figures, for instance, no longer command. We are sullen with our teachers or rowdy with our police, and both command so little respect from society that we pay them abysmally. God himself, once upon a time a commanding figure, is not so now. And parents know very well about the erosion of respect.

God first, for at least three reasons: fuller life, better life, ordered life. When we are under divine orders, it is entirely conceivable that our own lives will be, at last, in order. "This is the great and first commandment."

II

"And a second is like it. You shall love your neighbor as yourself." God first, other people second.

Again we see Christ's uniqueness. The commandment is not unique. It, too, is straight out of the Hebrew Scriptures. What is unique is Christ's repeated emphasis that the two go together. One or another Jewish leader may have coupled the two commands before Jesus, but none of them did it so consistently or thoroughly as he. It is his coupling which has survived, not theirs.

What Jesus did was what any great leader does. He sliced through the peripheral to the central. He went to the heart of the matter. He reminded the people of their priorities. The priorities were already there. They were in the Scriptures. But the forest had long ago been missed for the trees. What Jesus did was to give them the forest back.

A theology, Jesus was saying in effect, is no good without a sociology. A thinking man's love of God must be proved by his love of man. "Faith without works is dead." The two go hand in hand. They are indissoluble. The minute you try to split them apart you are in trouble.

This was the trouble in which the first-century Jews found themselves. And it is, again, unfair to excoriate them without including ourselves. This is the trouble in which a thinking man finds himself. While he may honestly feel that he loves God, he does not always see that love being proved in his love of other people.

This, of course, renders his vaunted honesty suspect. For if Jesus is saying that a theology is worthless without an ethic, he is also saying that an ethic may be unlikely without a theology. That is to say, *unless* we love God, we may very likely *not* love other people, at least not to the extent of loving the ones who are unlovely and certainly not to the extent of loving the ones who are our enemies.

It is most instructive that the great twin-priority passage in Luke is immediately followed by the story of the Good Samaritan. "Who is my neighbor?" the lawyer, a thinking man, asked Jesus. And Jesus, in effect, told him that his enemy was his neighbor—a bold idea since the rabbis had almost uniformly interpreted "Love your neighbor" as referring only to their fellow Jews. The beaten Jew was spurned, however, both by a priest and by an assistant priest—and Jesus no doubt chose them as exemplars of those who honestly felt, and said, that they loved God. But the beaten man was not neglected by the enemy who, incidentally, worshiped the same God. In other words, it was the enemy who had the priorities right—*both* priorities.

Christian love is enemy love. "Love God," St. Augustine said, "and do as you please." It is a profound statement. If a thinking man *really* loves God, he *will* love other people, even people who do not love him. Jesus' life was the proof. The lives of Christians should be the proof. Christian love, writes a commentator, is "the kind of love which seeks the good of *all* men under *all* circumstances."[1]

The priority is all. God first, others second. If God is not first, others may not be second. They may be last—as they were in "Christian" Germany, as they were in first-century Palestine, as they often are in our own communities. If we do not love God, it is entirely possible, even probable, that we will not love people who are not especially lovable.

> It it only when we love God that man becomes lovable. The Biblical teaching about man is . . . that man is made in the image of God (Gen. 1:26, 27). It is for that reason that man is lovable. The true basis of all democracy is in fact the love of God. Take away the love of God and we can become angry at man the unteachable [and] pessimistic about man the unimprovable.[2]

III

Self third. It is not a commandment. It is not that important. It is more an acknowledgment that the self is in the picture somewhere. There are only two commandments. "On these *two* commandments depend all the law and the prophets." However, the second commandment did say, "You shall love your neighbor *as yourself*."

The curious thing is that the self is given such short shrift by Jesus. It is the opposite of what the thinking

---

[1] Donald G. Miller, *Luke*, The Layman's Bible Commentary, vol. 18 (Richmond: John Knox, 1959), p. 105 (ital. added).

[2] William Barclay, *The Gospel of Matthew*, vol. 2 (Philadelphia: Westminster, 1958), p. 303.

man normally does. As we have seen, the priority scale for most of us reads: self first, others second, God third. And this is why we do not like the Bible. It is an affront to our egos. It puts the self last. We want to put the self first. It is a major reorientation.

But the self is so unimportant that there is no third commandment, Love yourself. It is so unimportant that, of sixteen commentaries on the twin-priority passages, only one has anything to say about it. And what that commentator says is this:

> This quotation from the Old Testament . . . probably does not represent the way in which [Jesus] would have described the love of neighbor . . . if he had been discussing it without reference to the traditional law.[3]

The way Jesus would have described it, the scholar suggests, is in the terms which he used just before the priority passage in Luke: "If any man would come after me, let him deny himself." There is not even the hint of self-love in that.

We say that you cannot possibly love other people, let alone God, unless you love yourself. Jesus is saying that you cannot love other people, let alone yourself, unless you love God. There is all the difference between those two positions. It is the difference between God first and self first, between what Jesus is saying and what a thinking man may be saying. And it just may be that Jesus, whose ideas have been around longer than the thinking man's, may be right and the thinking man wrong.

What thinking men are tempted to say is not that God is dead, not even that he is irrelevant, but that he is third. And that is a very serious thing to be saying about God. When the ancient Jews, in their "modern"

---

[3] John Knox, Exposition of Luke in *The Interpreter's Bible*, ed. G. A. Buttrick et al., vol. 8 (New York: Abingdon, 1952), p. 194.

way, said it, they invariably got into serious trouble. The prophets did all they could to get the people to turn back. So did Jesus. But they would not.

"The basic problem of modern man," says Arnold Toynbee, who ought to know, "is the worship of self." It has been the problem of "modern man" in every age. He has put self first and God third rather than God first and self third. He has not really done his homework, in other words, in fuller living, better living, and ordered living.

What we must do, then, is find out for ourselves which way makes more sense. We should, of course, be able to find out from a simple reading of history, the same way Toynbee found out. But most of us do not read history well. We seem to lack the imagination to apply to ourselves what happened to others. We have to experience it rather than imagine it. This makes for some pretty grim pessimism. "He who does not remember the past," wrote Santayana, "is condemned to repeat it." "We learn from history," said the German poet Heine, "that we do not learn from history."

Nevertheless, incredible as it may seem, we have, Christianity says, one thing going for us. This passage and another in Luke are the only ones in the synoptic gospels which speak of man's love for God.[4] Christianity's main point is God's love for man. "We love, because he first loved us." "For God so loved the world that he gave his only Son."

In other words, God is working with us to set the priorities. And the Man who reminded us of them is the proof.

---

[4] Vincent Taylor, *The Gospel According to St. Mark* (London: Macmillan, 1959), p. 487.

A Thinking Man's

Children

I

Why does a thinking man teach his children religion?

First, because he wants to. A thinking man by definition wants to teach. He is so caught up by the excitement of thinking that he wants to pass along his excitement to his children. His excitement is of two kinds—about the activity of thinking itself, and about the thoughts the activity produces.

Thus when a thinking man approaches religion he is as stimulated by his intellective activity there as he is by his intellective activity on his job. If he is not so stimulated then he is not, in the fullest sense, a thinking man. A thinking man, by definition, is one who is stimulated to think in the three great areas of life—that of the self, the psychological; that of others, the sociological; and that of God, the theological.

The thinking man then becomes so excited about what he discovers in the three areas that he wants to communicate it to his children. He has found, for instance, as he explores the third dimension, that there are some big thoughts that use him. That there is, possibly, a God. That that God writes his story in suffering love. That the suffering love is of a people and of a person and, incredible as it may seem, it is the

suffering love of people like the thinking man and
his children.

Because the thinking man is so caught up with ideas
like these he *wants* to pass them on to his children. It is
impossible to live in a house with two or six other
people and not pass along our excitements to them.
What is more, the thinking man does not simply let the
excitement percolate, he sets up conditions for it to
percolate. He is that caught up with it himself. And he
wants to be sure that his children are too. It is
that important to him.

Second, a thinking man teaches his children
religion because he wants to learn. A thinking man
by definition wants to learn.

In most of our church schools we have the entire
setup backwards. We spend all our time teaching our
children and almost none of it teaching their parents.
Such an emphasis is not only misguided, it is suicidal.
Our religion cannot be carried on by our children if we,
their parents, do not know what we are talking about.
We cannot know what we are talking about unless we
study. Fortunately, thinking men and thinking women
want to study. They remember that Jesus blessed the
children and taught the adults.

Third, a thinking man teaches his children religion
because he realizes that one of the best ways for the
teaching-learning process to take place is for the
participants to learn together. When we learn together
what neither of us knew to begin with, it is a memorable
moment. Fortunately, there is ample opportunity for
such moments in religion, since the knowledge of
parents does not greatly exceed that of their children.

The trouble with learning together, however, is that, by the time we are thirty, our defenses are up. Either we feel we have learned all we need to know to function successfully in the third area; or we defend ourselves by saying, "It's an important area, all right, but I just simply do not have the time to go into it in any depth." In other words, by the time we are thirty, we are either infallible or lazy.

Naturally, for learning together to take place, we must be intelligent enough, thoughtful enough, "thinking" enough, to get rid of our defenses. And I daresay we do. Most of us are probably already sitting down with our children and learning the new math or the new social studies unit or reading with them the new biography of Andrew Jackson or Lafayette. This kind of thing goes on in families all the time. And it is not only memorable. It is fun.

Fourth, a thinking man teaches his children religion because it is his business to. Just as there are certain things expected of him in his job, so there are certain things expected of him in his home. If he is in the Judeo-Christian tradition, then he is expected to teach his children the Judeo-Christian tradition. There is nothing permissive about it, nothing voluntary. These are his *orders*. He is under obligation to pass his religion on to his children. "These words which I *command* you this day shall be upon your heart; and you *shall* teach them diligently to your children."

It wasn't too long ago that most Christian families considered Sunday Schools an insult. If you had to send your child to Sunday School it meant that he wasn't being taught anything in his home. Sunday Schools were for children without homes or with non-Christian parents. But if a Christian parent sent his child to Sunday School, it meant he wasn't doing his job.

There has never, in the Judeo-Christian tradition, been any pussyfooting around about who teaches the children religion. "You shall teach your children." And those fathers did. They taught their children so well that they, in turn, taught their children, and so on, down the line, to the point where, it is quite possible, we are in or out of the tradition now because of the way in which our fathers taught us and their fathers taught them. "You shall teach your children."

Why do thinking men teach their children religion? Because they want to teach, they want to learn, they want to learn with their children, and, just as in their jobs, they want to obey their orders.

II

The other question is not Why but How do we teach our children? Desire is one thing, action another. We can have all the desire in the world, but without the thought to put that desire into action, it will be worth little.

· Many thinking people are frustrated in getting from Why to How. We can all agree, perhaps, on the desirability of parents educating their children in things religious, but then when it comes to sitting down on the sofa and doing the educating, we just don't come through. We say we don't have the time, which is not true. We say let the church school do it, which is impossible. We say we don't know how, which is unthinking.

Fortunately we have the following excellent guides for teaching our children religion. There is nothing particularly new or mysterious about them. They have been around for a long time. Recently they were codified in a remarkable little book called "Powerful Learning Tools in Religion," written by the Union College Character Research Project, and available to thinking families for only one dollar. These are the basic steps in teaching our children religion.

Step One: Reserve the time. Research shows that the best time is two days after the presentation of the original material. If that presentation takes place on Sunday morning in the church school rather than in the home, then the time for a thinking man to begin to teach his children is Tuesday. Before dinner, after dinner, during dinner, before bed—any time, the right time, Tuesday.

Step Two: Focus on one main point. This is the goal for the lesson. "If you teach one thing well," say the Character Research people, "children may learn it. If you teach four things, they will probably not learn any of them, no matter how well you teach."

Now a goal to be helpful must, according again to research, have the following characteristics: One, it must be attainable. Can my child *do* it? It must not be out of reach. And it must not be vague. It is vague to ask your ten-year-old boy, who is studying the lives of famous Old Testament figures, "How did God help his heroes?" It is clear to ask, "How did Abraham Lincoln depend on God?"

Two, the goal must not only be attainable, it must be verifiable. Can my child *see* it? When he has carried it out, can both he and I see how much he has learned?

Is progress evident? The goal "bring back some facts about your Sunday School teacher" does not produce as much verifiable progress as the goal, "bring back two facts about your Sunday School teacher."

Three, the goal must be challenging. Will it bring out my child's *best*? The emphasis is twofold: *my* child, with his particular characteristics, and my child's *best*, his top performance. It is not challenging to give your twelve-year-old daughter the goal, "List some qualities of people you like and some of people you don't like." It is challenging to set this goal with your daughter: "Find the best way you can help a disruptive classmate make a positive contribution to the group and report back next Tuesday."

Four, the goal must be *written*. It should be one sentence, preferably in the form of a question, using the first person, with a carbon or at least a copy, one for the parent and one for the child. Otherwise our goals will be vague and we will be hard put to verify our progress. This way we will have a record and our pencils will, as they usually do, clarify our thoughts.

Step Three: After we have reserved the time and focused on one main point, we make every effort to coordinate the learning with the life. We are teaching a child with particular wants and needs and frustrations. We must relate what he learns to *his* life, not just to "life," which is vague, or he will not learn it.

This is called situation teaching. It goes from the situation to the principle, not vice versa. It is the inductive method: from the specific to the general, from the phenomenon to the hypothesis, and not vice versa.

If the need of a ten-year-old boy is to have heroes, as

it is for nearly all ten-year-old boys, and if a thinking man's son is particularly excited by American heroes, as most American sons are, and if his boy is also particularly excited by Abraham Lincoln, then he asks him the question about Abraham Lincoln and works from there to God. You do not work from God to Abraham Lincoln to your son. You work from your son to Abraham Lincoln to God. And there is all the difference between those two techniques.

The inductive method requires imagination and patience. It is not easy. It requires imagination in setting the goal, and it requires patience in reaching it. You could tell your son in five seconds: "Abraham Lincoln depended on God." But it may take a week for your son to discover for himself, through various readings and discussions with you, that Abraham Lincoln depended on God. It is, however, worth the work of imagining and being patient. This way you learn, the other way you recite. The one way is a thinking man's, the other not.

Incidentally, it should be pointed out that the inductive method of teaching is one of the oldest and possibly the best. Socrates taught not by pontificating principles but by asking questions and then leading his pupils, with imagination and patience, to discover the principles for themselves.

Step Four: Reinforce the learning. Set up "cues" to be worked on through the week. A toothbrush, for instance, can be a cue to a kindergartener who is learning we are God's helpers when we care for our bodies. Cues come up all the time for children in classes trying to relate to unruly friends or impatient and unimaginative teachers. The question is not, "Can you repeat the Golden Rule?" The goal of the lesson is, "What way can you think of to apply the Golden Rule in your relationship with your algebra teacher, whom you can't stand?" Similar goals work, of course, for parents in *their* relationships.

Step Five: Review at stated intervals. The intervals are as follows: two days later, as we have seen, five days after that, ten days after that, and twenty days after that. This is the way we make our learning permanent. Nothing is so impermanent as the learning stuffed into the head at the last minute for the exam. On the other hand, few things are so permanent as regularly reviewed material. "We tell students," say the Character Research people, "if you use this method conscientiously, you will never get a grade lower than B."

A thinking man has his motivation. He wants to teach, he wants to learn, he wants to learn with his children, he knows he has his orders to teach them. And, because he is a thinking man, he knows *how* to convert his desire into action and get in there and teach.

A Thinking Man's

Miracle

"I don't believe in the miracles. Therefore I can't be a Christian. Or if I am one I'm not a very good one." It is a familiar refrain.

Axeheads float, sticks turn into snakes, walls crumble to trumpets, the sun stands still, a sea is parted, a storm is calmed, water is turned into wine, four thousand people are fed by seven loaves and a few small fish.

It's all in the Bible—nature miracles, healing miracles, resurrection miracles. And the question to a thinking man is: Do I have to believe them to be a Christian? To be specific: Do I have to believe that Jesus walked on water to believe in Jesus?

I

The best way to answer that question is to begin by putting it in perspective. And one way to do that is to remind ourselves of several things miracles are not.

For one thing, miracles are *not* central. A thinking man's faith does not depend upon them. They were constantly underplayed by Jesus. He told people not to talk about them. He refused to perform them for his own good. He would not use them to call attention to himself. He would not use them with people who asked for them but had no faith.

By the same token, miracles are *not* peripheral. They are not late. They are not added. They are referred to by Jesus. He uses them in his teaching. Virtually all of them come from eyewitness accounts. They cannot therefore be written off as unimportant. A thinking man must come to grips with miracles.

For a third thing, the Bible's miracles are *not* unique. Although they would appear to be better attested than those in other religions, the fact remains that other religions have them.[1] Buddha was said to have made floods recede, healed wounds, passed through walls, walked on water. Lao Tse was said to have raised the dead. In these and other religions storms cease, the sun stops, food appears, events are foretold, thoughts are divined, demons are routed, the sick are cured, the dead raised. Specifically, the walking on the water, the stilling of the storm, the feeding of the four thousand and others, "closely resemble," a scholar tells us, "the miracle stories current in the Greco-Roman world of the first century."[2]

A fourth thing miracles are *not* is comprehensible. They cannot, strictly speaking, be rationalized. They are there, and they have to be dealt with, but they cannot be dealt with in the usual way. It is hard to rationalize them in, and it is hard to rationalize them out.

For instance, if we try to rationalize them in, the argument goes like this. A miracle is not contrary to the laws of nature, it is contrary to what we know about

---

[1] J. A. MacCulloch in *Encyclopedia of Religion and Ethics,* ed. J. Hastings, vol. 7 (New York: Scribner's, 1928), p. 678.

[2] F. C. Grant in *The Interpreter's Bible,* ed. G. A. Buttrick et al., vol. 7 (New York: Abingdon, 1951), p. 708.

the laws of nature. Therefore an exception to the law is theoretically possible and Jesus could have walked on water. Put another way, "With God all things are possible," even what appear to be the most flagrant violations of natural law.

Or we can try to rationalize miracles out. That argument goes like this: (1) the Bible writers had to compete with the magical claims of other religions; (2) they miraculized events we would not consider miraculous today, especially the psychosomatic healing miracles; (3) they simply exaggerated to make their point, much as product managers and advertising companies do today; (4) each miracle has some point of vulnerability—for example, walking on the water could be translated walking "by" the water, and is so translated at the end of John; calming the storm could have happened as coincidence, since storms ended as soon as they began on the capricious Sea of Galilee.

Most experts agree that neither rationalization quite works. Miracles cannot be explained nor can they be explained away. They are there and they have to be dealt with, but they do not have to be dealt with in the same way we deal with other problems that intrigue us as thinking men.

II

The answer seems to lie in switching gears. Once we have gotten miracles in perspective, we can proceed to deal with them in the only way in which they will ever "make sense," namely by recovering the humanity in them. This is, of course, the opposite of what we normally do. Normally we get so hung up on the divinity we forget the humanity. We miss the point as we flail around on the subpoint. We mistake the end for the means. The end is that the miracle is there to say something about *me*. The means is the story. But I should never get so exercised by the story that I forget the history.

Truth is what works for me by explaining me to myself. Now that is not all truth is, but truth is at least that, particularly in religion. Religion is *self*-centered. If it were not self-centered it wouldn't work. It wouldn't last. It wouldn't "mean" anything. The *point* of religion is to explain me to myself. It is to give me a frame of reference so I can make things fit.

The astonishing thing is that the miracles in the Bible fit. If they didn't fit they wouldn't speak to me. They do fit. They work. They explain me to myself. They help me discover my humanity.

The *point* of Jesus' walking on the water is not that Jesus walked on water. How could anybody do that? How could Jesus not do that? It's a standoff. It can't be rationalized one way or the other. You think you have it, and then you don't, like mercury from a broken thermometer. It's impossible? But then why do you belong to a church, since the church is founded on the biggest miracle, the resurrection? It's possible? But then how do you explain the fact that it hasn't happened again? It's a standoff.

The *point* of Jesus' walking on the water is not that Jesus walked on water. How could that be the point when he never let them make it the point? He never even mentions it. Nobody brings it up. Nobody. Ever. If it had happened, they would never have stopped mentioning it. If it had not happened, would they have stayed with Jesus and would we be here today?

The *point* of Jesus' walking on the water is not that Jesus walked on water. It is that *I* am struggling; *I* am afraid; *my* faith is weak; *something* is there. *Peter* is the point of the miracle, not Jesus. Jesus is the *means* to Peter's self-development. The miracle is the *means* to my self-discovery.

But what if the miracle does not fit? Maybe I am not struggling; I am not afraid; my faith is strong; I need nothing. And this is the way I am, yes, much of the time. As a thinking man I am the "master of my fate, the captain of my soul." That is why I need the miracles to startle me back to reality. "Many were astonished at him." The word "miracle" comes from the word for "astonish." I need a story that is so utterly *un*fitting as a miracle, to startle me back to self-discovery.
But the Bible doesn't stop at miracles. It will use any means to help explain a man to himself. Sagas, dramas, legends, poetry, short stories, myths. Any means are legitimate to the end of jarring a man to come to grips with himself. And the miracles are the most jarring means of all.

But what have you done? You are back trying to rationalize. To humanize the miracles is to rationalize them away. You can buy any miracle in the Bible now so long as you can discover the human element in it. And every miracle, obviously, is vulnerable to that search. You recover the human, in other words, and lose the divine.

But do you? Or do you discover the divine, really discover it, for the first time? Where can the divine *be* if it is not in the human? If God is not in my struggle, where *is* he? If he is not in my fear, where *is* he?

If he is not in my lack of faith—as Israel's in the exodus and Peter's with Jesus—where *can* he *be*?

The point is not that we have explained away the divine. It is that the divine, because miracles are so startling, long ago explained away the human. Now with the recovery of the human in the Bible we can begin to recover the divine. God *is* what is with me as I doubt and fear my way to be what it is in me to be. And whenever God is, that is miracle.

All right. But doesn't that subjectivize truth unduly? You are saying that the miracle may or may not have happened. The important thing is that it happens to you. You bet. That is precisely what I am saying. And I am saying it for two reasons: One, because the thirty-five miracles of Jesus just simply cannot be proved or disproved. They can be believed or disbelieved, but they cannot be proved or disproved. It all depends on your assumption. If your belief is in the regularity and inviolability of nature, then miracles are not for you. But that does not prove or disprove miracles. It only says miracles are not for you because they do not square with your belief in the laws of nature. If your belief, on the other hand, is in the regularity and inviolability of God, then miracles may very well be for you. God could do with any of his laws what he wished. But note: this is faith vs. faith, it is not proof vs. proof. It is a matter of whether you are working from a naturalistic or theistic hypothesis. That is, which one helps things fit better for you as a thinking man? Miracles *depend* on faith just as they do in the New Testament. Miracles *depend* on me.

Two, the important thing is that the miracle happens to me because, in religion, "truth *is* subjectivity."[3] God means *nothing* apart from his meaning something to *me*. It is no good to say that God exists but that his existence means nothing to me. That is an impossible, self-contradictory statement in religion. If God exists, then he exists for me, and I am passionately involved in his existence.

It could well be argued that most of our troubles with religion have come from our eagerness to objectify it. We were not content to say this is the way it is for me. We went on to say this is the way it has to be for you. That is what the Inquisition did. That is what the Crusades did. That is what we do now when we imperialize someone else to believe as we believe.

Religion is not subjective enough. It rarely has been. The reason the Bible lasts is that it is a compilation of radically subjective statements. The prophets experienced God with passionate inwardness. So did Jesus. So did Moses. So did the patriarchs. The *only* advances in religion come when men of lonely walking fear and doubt their way to be what it is in them to be. Read Coretta King's biography of her husband, and let the miracle of it burn into you.

Ah, you object, but there is a danger to all this inwardness. And you are right. The danger is that we will become so selfish we will not be selfless. We will become so intent on what religion has to tell us about ourselves that we will forget what it tells us about other selves. We will remember that religion is self-centered

[3] Søren Kierkegaard, *Concluding Unscientific Postscript*, trans. Walter Lowrie (Princeton: Princeton University Press, 1944), p. 169 (ital. added).

but forget that it is also *other*-centered. We will remember "as yourself" in Jesus' command but forget "love your neighbor."

It is a real danger. And we are seeing it in the Jesus cult and the drug cult and the return of the astral religions. But there are ways to avoid such excessive subjectivization. One is to read and reread the Bible. It is to saturate ourselves with stories like this. It is to be so astounded by the miraculous that we begin to recover the human.

But how does that differ from humanism? The humanist is trying to recover our common humanity too. The answer has to be in the symbols. For one thing, you would rarely find a humanist in the Bible. He would go elsewhere for his stories—to Abraham Lincoln, Gandhi, perhaps even Jesus as a great man.

But would that be enough? Is a mere scrutiny of history enough, or is there something more in the sacred history of the Judeo-Christian tradition? It may be that there *is* nothing more. And there are many who say that the tradition is bankrupt and the proof is its lack of impact on the agony of our time.

There are others, however, and they are in churches by definition, who would say that *something* is in that tradition, and it may be the hope of the world. Consider, they say, such things as the miracles. There *is* something objective about them as well as subjective. And the objective thing is power. Indeed, that is the word most often used in the Bible to describe the miracles. It is the word Jesus used.[4] They were called "acts of power."

---

[4] B. W. Grundmann in *Theological Dictionary of the New Testament*, ed. G. Kittel, vol. 2 (Grand Rapids: Eerdmans, 1964), p. 301.

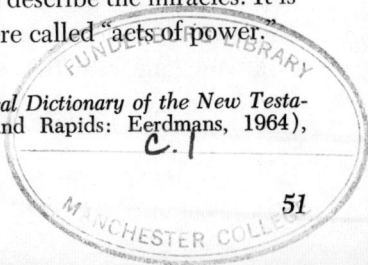

I never cease to be amazed at the millions of thinking people who turn out every week to read these stories. What is it in the sagas and legends and miracles and dramas that compels such allegiance? Do you find that many people going that often to meetings of their political party? Of any other organization in the country? You do not. We can only conclude that the power in the stories in the tradition is greater than the power in the stories of the country.

As a matter of fact, the power is so great that it is frightening. Moses was terrified at the burning bush. "When the disciples saw him walking on the sea, they were terrified. . . . And they cried out for fear." "Terror" was another word for "miracle."

The power is so great you can't believe it. "O man of little faith," Jesus said to Peter, "why did you doubt?" You are not *expected* to believe in the miracles. What will happen is that the reality to which they point is so *powerful* that over two and three thousand years you will be moved by it, it will be you.

But that is not the end. Startling as it may seem, you may even find yourself doing what you felt but could not think. "He who believes in me will *also* do the works that I do; and *greater* works than these will he do." It is astounding. But it is there. It has to be dealt with. "Energy," "act," "erg" were other words for "miracle."

These ancient symbols are unbelievably powerful for thinking men. They are terrifyingly accurate. They explain me to myself, and they compel me to do for others what I never thought I could do. In a word, they evince my humanity. In a word, they *are* God. God *is* the name we give that power.

A Thinking Man's

Sin

"I don't believe in original sin. It is one of those things in the Bible I just can't buy. Men are not that bad."

Maybe so. Maybe not. The important thing for the thinking man is to find out what the doctrine says and then whether it fits.

Basically it says these things.

I

One, sin is distance. There are many other things you can say about sin, but this is one that includes many. I am distant from God. I am distant from other people. I am distant from myself.

Consider God. The ancient Jew lived in a theocentric world. He began with God. We live in an anthropocentric world. We begin with man. God *was* what the ancient Jew was separated from. The word "holy" came from the root for "separate." Sin was distance from God first. "Against thee, thee only have I sinned."

Consider other people. They were supposed to be close and yet they were distant. The distance was called injustice. Sin is what I do to you that isn't you. And it was going on everywhere.

The weak you have not strengthened, the sick you have not healed, the crippled you have not bound up, the

strayed you have not brought back, the lost you have
not sought.

Consider the distance between a man and himself.
Sin is what I do to myself that isn't me. It was happening
all the time.

> I know my transgressions,
>> and my sin is ever before me.
>
> "Woe is me! For I am lost: for I am a man of unclean lips."
>
> "I do not do what I want, but I do the very thing I hate."

Two, sin is universal. Everybody is far from himself,
far from other people, far from God. That is the meaning
of the word "original." The myth had it that the first man
sinned. Consequently everyone after the first man sinned.
It was an old way of saying that distance is a fact of
life. "The sins of the fathers are visited on the children."
It was an old way of saying not that the children were
responsible for their fathers' misdeeds, which would be
absurd, but that the children were bound to be distant
just as their fathers were.

To be *is* to be distant. I am not who I could be. I am
not a man for others. I am not a man for God. That was
the point of the myths. It was the point of the stories.
It was the point of the prophecies and the psalms.
They were not theories about life, they were
descriptions.

> There is no man who does not sin.
>
> There is not a righteous man on earth.
>
> All men have sinned and fall short of the glory of God.
>
> There is none that does good. . . .
> They have all gone astray, they are
>> all alike corrupt;
>> there is none that does good,
>> no, not one.

Or, if you prefer it from nonreligious sources: "What history does," writes historian Herbert Butterfield, "is . . . to uncover man's universal sin."[1] "The doctrine of original sin," writes a commentator in the London *Times,* "is the only empirically verifiable doctrine of Christian faith."[2]

Three, sin is radical. It goes to the "root" of personality. Indeed, man is *more* bad than good. We may not like that but that is where the Bible comes out. At the very least, man is fifty-one percent bad. "The good that I would I do not." A saint said that.

> *Every* imagination of the thoughts of his heart was *only* evil *continually.*

That's strong language, but that is the way the Bible reads the evidence. And after fifty million people dead from wars in this century alone, we are hard put to controvert that reading.

The Bible takes a dim view of human nature. Its first story ends in a murder and its last story, the story of Jesus, ends in a murder.

> The heart is deceitful above all things [wrote Jeremiah] and desperately corrupt.

> It is essential [writes our historian] not to have faith in human nature.[3]

Now, we may want to disagree. We may want to say that man is fifty-one percent good. That may be our reading of the evidence. It may come from our

[1] Herbert Butterfield, *Christianity and History* (New York: Scribner's, 1950), p. 45.

[2] Quoted by K. W. Thompson, "Christianity and Crisis," *Times* (London), 12 June 1967.

[3] Butterfield, *Christianity and History,* p. 47.

experience and from our American idealism. "In every day and in every way," Russell Conwell chirped in the last century, "we are getting better and better." But that is not a biblical sentiment.

> How can a man be just before God [Job asks]?
>
> Behold, I was brought forth in iniquity,
>   and in sin did my mother conceive me.

It meant that the distance was in his roots and that his life was *more* distance than it was union.

> All of mankind since Adam has been sinful, . . . the *whole* man is sinful, . . . man's *entire* life is sinful from its beginning.[4]
>
> My sin [wrote the psalmist] is *ever* before me.
>
> Wretched man that I am [wrote the saint]!

Four, sin is willful. I will it. I do it. I am responsible for it. I cannot pass the responsibility to my mother, my father, my country, or my God. It is my choice, my decision, in my freedom.

The heart was the seat of sin for the Hebrew. It was the seat of the will. The word for "heart" was synonymous with the word for "will." Man willed his self-destruction. He willed injustice. He willed his atheism.

> They did not obey or incline their ear, but everyone walked in the stubbornness of his evil heart.

If sin is universal, how can it be willful? If it is radical, how can it be willful? If I am bound to sin, how can I be responsible for sinning? You *are* responsible, the Bible says, and there is no exit from your responsibility. You are bound to be distant, but you

---

[4] S. J. DeVries in *The Interpreter's Dictionary of the Bible,* ed. G. A. Buttrick et al., vol. 4 (New York: Abingdon, 1962), p. 365 (ital. added).

choose to be distant. "I do," said the saint, "the very thing I hate." He was bound to sin, but he chose to sin.

Five, therefore sin is punishable. We call the punishment guilt. Guilt is distance felt. It is the feeling of distance. It is what I feel between you and me. It is what I feel between me and myself. It is what I feel between me and God.

The idea of sin in the Bible always includes its results.[5] The penalty follows immediately and necessarily.

> He who digs a pit will fall into it, and a stone will come back upon him who starts it rolling.

The penalty is not pleasant.

> My iniquities . . . weigh like a burden too heavy for me.

> I am utterly bowed down and prostrate;
>   all the day I go about mourning.

> My punishment is more than I can bear.

The question, therefore, at this point is whether there is an exit from guilt or whether our punishment, as Cain's, will be more than we can bear.

Six, sin is inescapable. There is no escape, there is no exit, *on our own.* It is one of the great insights of the Bible. Jesus' greatest wrath was reserved for those who thought they could bridge their own distances. It can't be done.

There is a war in the Bible, and it is the saint's word, which means there is a war in us, between those saying the distances can be bridged and those saying they cannot. More accurately: a man tries to bridge his own distances; he fails; then he realizes he needs help.

---

[5] Ibid., p. 367.

Guilt is not negative. It is essential to the building of a man. It moves a man to try to build his own bridges, to try anything that will overcome the distances between himself and God and other people. Then a man is ready for God.

The Bible is loaded with symbols of man's defiance, of his fierce pride that he can be the man he was meant to be, that he can be for others, that he can be for God. Sin *is* willful, and I *will* love, I *will* believe, I *will* be at peace with myself.`

The first symbol was in the Garden. Man would do on his own what he could not do on his own. The second was in the Tower of Babel. "Nothing," reads the story, "that they propose to do will now be impossible for them." The third symbol was Abraham's flight to Egypt, attempting to overcome the distances he felt on his own. And so it goes throughout the entire Bible, which is to say throughout our lives. It is the necessary pilgrim's progress.

A man has to rise before he can fall. Indeed, he rises *in order* to fall. He has to try to bridge the distance before the distance can be bridged. He has to be proud before he can be humble. He has to try to save himself before he can learn he cannot save himself.

That is why the constant movement in the Bible is to bring a man down. It is to humble him. It is to humiliate him. It is to break him.

> The sacrifice acceptable to God is
> a broken spirit.

It was so utterly unacceptable to a *thinking man* who came later that he tacked on an ending. No *thinking man* wants to be broken.

> They have no pangs;
>> their bodies are sound and sleek. . . .
> Pride is their necklace. . . .
> Truly thou dost set them in slippery places.

That was the point. So they would fall. A man *has* to slip.

> Though you soar aloft like the
>> eagle,
> though your nest is set among
>> the stars,
> thence I will bring you down,
>> says the Lord.

God *is* what brings a man down.

Seven, sin *is* escapable *with help*. Sin is distance. Guilt is distance felt. Grace is distance overcome.

But it isn't that easy. Again there is an argument in the Bible, which is to say there is an argument in us. Is grace free or is it conditioned? Is there something I have to *do* to *earn* grace, or is grace *given* me *regardless* of what I do?

Confusing as it is, we have to answer that grace is, according to the Bible, both free and conditioned. On the one hand, Israel is freely chosen and Jesus freely given. On the other hand, there are certain things the Israelites and the followers of Jesus must do if their distances are to be overcome. A thinking man will not let go that easily. He has to do *some* building, even if it gets him only one percent of the way. The airplane takes you two thousand miles. But it does not pick you up at your home. You have to drive the twenty miles to the airport.

A first condition of distance overcome is that we admit the distance is there. It is easy to delude ourselves into thinking it is not. This is the sin of complacency, of unadmitted distance. "The greatest of sins," said

Carlyle, "is to be conscious of none." It is what we might call the Eichmann factor in each of us.

> I have nothing to confess [Adolf Eichmann, the Nazi war criminal, said before his death]. I have not sinned. I am clear with God. . . . I did nothing wrong. I have no regrets.[6]

A second condition of distance overcome is that we admit the distance remains. It is equally easy to delude ourselves into thinking we have overcome distance when we haven't. This is what we might call the Pharisee factor in each of us. The Pharisees set up an elaborate system of rules which, if followed, would bridge the gap between themselves and God and others. It didn't. No system can. Not capitalism. Not democracy. Not Christianity. The distance remains. It is the height of man's monstrous egoism to think any system can bridge the gap. We must be brought down from that kind of thinking, which is the one good thing that has come out of Vietnam, that the giant has been humbled.

A third condition of distance overcome is that we want it to be overcome. The word the Bible used was "Repent." It was the first word Jesus used in his preaching. It was the word the first church took in their preaching. You feel the distance so much that you are moved to want it overcome. "My soul thirsts for thee like a parched land." It is to want the distance overcome that much.

A fourth condition of distance overcome is that we fail at trying to overcome it. Only then can we understand the deep meaning of repentance. It is not only that we repent for having chosen distance. It is that

---

[6] Quoted by George Cornell, *Minneapolis Star,* 9 March 1963.

we repent for having tried to overcome that distance on our own.

A final condition of distance overcome is that we accept the forgiveness we begin to feel.

> I said, "I will confess my transgressions
>   to the Lord";
> *then* thou didst forgive the guilt
>   of my sin.

The forgiveness begins to be felt in the confession, which was the first two conditions.

> If we confess our sins, he . . . will forgive our sins.

It continues to be felt in the repentance, which was the second two conditions.

> A baptism of repentance for the forgiveness of sins.

And now it is felt as we accept it.

It sounds easier than it is. A thinking man cannot believe his distances are being overcome. It is beyond belief. But it is not beyond experience. It is happening. "Shout for joy, all you upright in heart." Joy is the feeling of distance overcome. "It is good to be *near* the Lord."

> How can I give you up, O Ephraim!
>   How can I hand you over, O
>   Israel! . . .
> My compassion grows warm and
>   tender.

A thinking man is close to other people. He crosses the road, strengthens the weak, heals the sick, seeks the lost. The other, in the saint's words, is "the brother for whom Christ died." He accepts him. He no longer fights him. Because he feels he is accepted. God *is* what he feels accepted by.

He even accepts himself. It is unbelievable. But it is not unacceptable. It is happening. He is no longer at war with himself. He has begun his descent. The bridge is coming to him.

"I am," a man exulted. It was in his eyes. It was beautiful. "I have self-worth. I don't have to prove anything any more. Now I am free." And the joy of it, the nearness of it, flooded the room.

"Oh, I'm so happy," a teen-ager writes. "I had to tell someone who didn't already know." It was the Good News of how she had "accepted" the man in whom all distances had been overcome. "A great weight has been lifted from me, and I don't have to worry about myself any more."

We are far from God. We are far from other people. We are far from ourselves. Sin is distance. Guilt is distance felt. Grace is distance overcome. "Your sins are forgiven," he said. He is *near*. God *is* what is near. God *is* whenever my distance is overcome.

A Thinking Man

and the Atonement

When we say that the proof of God's grace is
Jesus Christ, what do we mean? When Paul wrote that
"God shows his love for us in that while we were yet
sinners Christ died for us," what did he mean? When a
thinking man hears that a man who died two thousand
years ago died for *him*, what does it mean?

I

The best way to understand the atonement is to
begin with the fact of man's estrangement. We are
strangers to God. No thinking man would say he could
not know God better. The ultimate in such theological
estrangement is called despair. So often we despair of
there being an ultimate meaning.

We are strangers to each other. No thinking man
would say he could not know other people better. The
ultimate in such sociological estrangement is war.
We are at war with our enemies. Sometimes we are at
war with our own countrymen. Often we are at war
in our own homes.

We are strangers to ourselves. No thinking man would
say he could not know himself better. "Know thyself"
was the inscription over the oracle at Delphos. But we
don't. The ultimate in such psychological estrangement
is schizophrenia, which means, literally, a "mind split."
But we are all split. It is only a matter of degree.

There is a split in most thinking men between who they are and the men they want to be.

The split, the estrangement, the separation, the hostility are all modern ways of describing what the Bible called "sin." "All have sinned," Paul wrote, "and fall short of the glory of God." Only the most naive idealist would disagree, and we have only to look into ourselves to see that his disagreement would be wrong.

Fact One, then, is that we are estranged.

II

Fact Two, according to the Christian faith, is that a thinking man's estrangement has been overcome. The Christian faith says that no matter how greatly we have sinned and fallen short of the glory of God, our sin has been forgiven. We are strangers, but our estrangement has been overcome. We are split from God, we are hostile to each other, we are estranged even from ourselves, but our split, our hostility, our estrangement, incredible as it may seem, have been overcome. So, too, our despair, hatred, and schizophrenia.

They have been overcome by Christ. This is the "good news" of the gospel. To tell anyone who despairs of ultimate meaning, or who is going through hell in his marriage, or is split off from the man he knows he should be that his despair, his hatred, and his schizophrenia have been lifted, is to tell him the best news he has ever heard in his life. "God shows his love for us in that while we were yet sinners Christ died for us." That is the Christian gospel. That is the atonement.

In Christ, the theory goes, God took the initiative and made us all "at one" with him, at one with each other, and at one with ourselves. That is what the word "atone" means. It means as it spells—to be "at one." When we are "at one" the big words come. Despair turns into hope, hatred into love, schizophrenia into integrity. We are whole now rather than split. We are united with God rather than divided. We are "close" to other people rather than "distant." "The fruit of the Spirit," Paul wrote, "is love, joy, peace, patience, kindness, goodness, faithfulness, gentleness, self-control." They are "at-one" words; none of them is "split-."

We all want to be at one. None of us wants to be split. A man at war with his wife wants to be at peace. A woman at war with her God wants to be at peace. A young person at war between who he is and who he wants to be longs for peace.

"He is our peace," says a New Testament writer referring to Christ. He is the one who has overcome our estrangement, healed our split, in the Bible's words "broken down the dividing wall of hostility." We are one at last and at war no more. That is the doctrine of the atonement.

III

But it is a long way from doctrine to experience, and Fact Two, that a thinking man's estrangement has been overcome by Christ, makes no sense—indeed, *is not a fact at all*—until it is believed, until, that is, a thinking man *says* it is a fact. *The* atonement must become *his* atonement. It cannot just "be true." It has to be true for *him*. Indeed, it is *not* true *until* it is true for him.

Now let's be honest. There are many thinking people who could not care less about the atonement and have no interest in seeing Fact Two completed in their own lives.

For one thing, they may view the atonement as incomprehensible. What possible sense could it make, they ask, to say that a man who died two thousand years ago died for me? It is logically incomprehensible. It is chronologically bizarre. Therefore, just as I leave the running of the government to the politicians and business to the management and war to the generals, so I leave theology to the theologians.

For another thing, many people may view the atonement as irrelevant. Granting it is possible, granting its credibility, even its desirability, it just does not have anything to say to me. I can lead a perfectly good life without it. What possible difference could it make to a woman at her sink that Christ died for her? The theory is of so little relevance as not to engage our minds.

The objections may be valid. Let's pursue the theory in an effort to root it in experience. The objections will stand or fall accordingly.

The theory is there whether we like it or not, and it is very likely to be there for another two thousand years. Any thinking man, therefore, will be challenged to come to grips with it, just as he has been challenged to come to grips with the theory of democracy and, if he is an American, generally has come to grips. The minute we come to grips with an idea of such magnitude, it is automatically no longer irrelevant. And the minute we remember that it is held by roughly one-third of the world, our criticism of it as incomprehensible may sound a trifle naive.

One thing is expected of the thinking man. One choice, one decision must be made. One work, if you will, must be undertaken. "What must I *do*," Paul's jailer asked, "to be saved?" "Believe in the Lord Jesus," Paul replied. A thinking man must make a choice: either he believes the atonement to be a fact, or he does not. Either it is true for him or it is not. And the only way to make that decision intelligently is, himself, to atone.

So many of us have the idea that belief is a matter of assent to intellectual propositions. But there is more to it. It is a matter of *living* those propositions to see whether or not they are validated in experience, which is a matter of *both* thinking and acting. We might even go so far as to say it is *more* a matter of acting than thinking. As has been seen, we can often act ourselves into a new way of thinking more readily than we think ourselves into a new way of acting.

Our actions, however, which put the theory to the test, are not going to be easy. They weren't for Christ and they aren't for us. The Christian life is not natural for a thinking man. When his boss swears at him, he has no desire to be at one with him. When his wife is petulant, he wants to be petulant back. When his children are demanding, he wants to get out of the house.

There is, then, only one way to try to do the atoning. Since it is unnatural, it has to be structured. It has to be impacted into our lives—into our datebooks and checkbooks. It has to be scheduled. To be atoned for *is* to atone. It is to do everything in our power to be at one with God, with others, and with ourselves. But we will *not* do everything in our power unless, self-consciously, every day, we schedule ourselves to do everything in our power. Then, when the crisis comes, we will be ready to respond as Christians.

Obviously this means some sort of discipline. Disciples are not made without discipline. Thinking men do not visit jails without discipline. It is too unnatural. It does too much violence to the normal way of running their lives. Therefore they have to solder onto their schedules people who are split apart from other people—and from themselves and from God—in jails, homes, jobs, schools, ghettoes.

IV

There are other questions. Why should we do it? Why should we atone in order to understand the atonement? Where is the motivation? We have said that the thinking man cannot help doing it, but isn't there more?

There is. And the more is that the atoning life can be better. It is not a choice between the bad life and the good. We do not want to make the mistake that many zealous evangelists make. For a thinking man it is a choice between the good life and a better one.

It can be more exciting to do something unnatural than natural. It can be more challenging to figure out how to love than to hate, hope than despair, integrate than fracture. It can be more adventurous to reach for the heights than be content with the plateaus. "A man's reach should exceed his grasp," Browning wrote, "or what's a heaven for?"

But can't you do all this without Christ? Anyone with even a modicum of intelligence knows it is better to be at one than estranged, to love than to hate, hope than despair, integrate than fracture. Why is Christ necessary to atone?

What Christ brought was a new dynamic. Obviously the Jews were challenged to atone. That is the point of their history. But it never seemed to work out. And certainly it never worked out beyond their own country. They had no dynamic for talking about being at one except among themselves. Jews, by their own admission, are not missionaries.

> The summons not to wait till they meet you in your sheltered and orderly path, but to go forth and seek out and redeem the sinner and the fallen, the passion to heal and bring back to God the wretched and the outcast —all this I do not find in Rabbinism; *that* form of love seems lacking.[1]

What about the other religions? There are more than twice as many Christians as any other world religion, many of which have been around much longer than Christianity. How do you explain that except by the new dynamic? The other religions just simply do not have the power that the Christian has with Christ. They do not have a man, or if they have one, or many, their men are not like Christ. There is something in that man—and you can argue forever what it is, and whether it is divine or human or both—there is something in that man that motivates people to *want* to atone, to do everything in *their* power to be at one with God and with other people and with themselves. Take away Christ and you take away the motivation.

What is expected of thinking men is that they become so involved in the despair and hate and schizophrenia of the world that a glimpse of the hope and love and wholeness of Christ may be caught, and we who are strangers to each other and to God and even to ourselves may be "at one" at last.

---

[1] C. G. Montefiore, quoted by C. H. Dodd in *The Epistle of Paul to the Romans*, The Moffatt New Testament Commentary (New York: Harper, 1932), p. 76.

A Thinking Man's

Requirements

Numerous attempts were made by the Jews to
summarize their law. The most famous was that of
Jesus when he condensed the six hundred thirteen laws
into two: love of God and love of neighbor. An earlier
attempt was that of Micah when he condensed the
laws into three so-called requirements.

> He has showed you, O man, what is good;
>   and what does the Lord require of you
> but to do justice, and to love kindness,
>   and to walk humbly with your God?

I

Four observations are in order before we look at
the requirements themselves.

First, the requirements sprang from controversy.
"The Lord has a controversy with his people," Micah said.
It was a legal term. It meant that God was bringing suit
against Israel. Why? Because Israel had questioned
God's leadership and the results, in Micah's opinion,
were dire. On the one hand, they had become
vulnerable to foreign attack. And on the other hand,
they were enjoying unparalleled domestic corruption.

The parallel is, of course, not difficult to draw.
A thinking man is vulnerable. The enemy may be death
or boredom or failure or simply "plateauing out" in his

middle years when he should have risen higher in the company than he did.

In any event, if we are vulnerable, Micah is suggesting, it is because we have questioned God's leadership. We have discussed his leadership when we should have obeyed. We have sat in our churches wondering who leads our lives, when we should have had the courage, and the humility, to be led. God's controversy with his people, in other words, is that they have made his requirements controversial.

A second observation is that God has already showed thinking men what is good. "He has *showed* you, O man, what is good." A thinking man, as we have seen, knows what the requirements are. Even if he does not believe in God, conscience has served him well. From parents, from society, from reason, from self-interest he has no doubt learned what the good is.

The trouble comes when we try to slip away from the demands of the good. We call the slipping rationalization. Rationalization makes gray what is often black and white. For example, we might say, "I am not paid what I am worth, so I am at liberty to make as much as I can from my expense account." Or, "It is very important that I get into college. If I don't my parents will be furious, and I won't be able to look at myself in the mirror. Therefore it is okay to bring along help for the exam."

The trouble also is that the thinking man may become arrogant about his knowledge of the good. He is such a long way from 700 B.C. when Micah lived, that he may well feel it is he who discovered the good rather than God who showed him the good. But if you take parents and society and reason and even self-interest all the way back, you will find this astonishing thought from Micah and the Jews before them. "*He* has showed you, O man, what is good." It does not read: "Congratulations, men, for having made the brilliant discovery that the following things are good."

A third observation, and it is a crucial one, is that what God showed thinking men was *good*. This is quite an assertion and one about which it is all too easy to be glib. When Micah says "good," he is deliberately not saying either of the good's two most serious philosophical and religious competitors, namely the true and the beautiful. "He has showed you, O man, what is good." Not "He has showed you, O man, what is true," nor "He has showed you, O man, what is beautiful."

The great contribution of the Jews was in ethics, not aesthetics. It was in morality, not philosophy. To be sure, the prophets and psalmists wrote beautiful poems, but the beauty was always for goodness. It was used to make the good desirable. Beauty was a means, never an end. In all Jewish history there is only one example of anything made that was exceptionally beautiful, namely the temple, and even that was ultimately destroyed and never rebuilt. And in all Jewish history there is not even one example of a philosopher. Beauty and truth were left to the Greeks.

Truth in this sense is not even mentioned in the earliest gospels—which is pretty amazing when you stop to think about it. The word "beauty" is used only twice in the entire New Testament. "Beauty is truth," Keats wrote, "truth beauty. That is all ye know on earth, and all ye need to know." That is a Greek sentiment, not a Judeo-Christian one. And it is not coincidental, of

course, that it is found in Keats's "Ode on a Grecian Urn."
It is a convincing summary of the Greek way of life.

An equally fine summary of the Judeo-Christian way
is from an old Presbyterian document. "Truth," wrote the
Presbyterians, "is in order to goodness." That is to say,
we know the truth in order to do the good. Truth without
goodness is worthless. The document did not even
mention beauty. Perhaps it should have. Calvinists have
often been criticized for being cheerless moralists. The
criticism and summary were both thrown into sharp
relief by Mark Twain when he described his first visit to
Virginia City, a town of sin, gambling, and whiskey:
"Virginia City," he said, "was certainly no place for a
Presbyterian—and I did not remain one very long."

A last observation is about the requirements
themselves. They are just that—requirements. "What
does the Lord *require* of you?" Not "What does the Lord
ask?" Not "What does the Lord suggest?" But "What
does the Lord require?"

The controversy really begins when thinking men turn
the requirements into suggestions. There is the
"trickle-down" theory of economics, which holds that if
the rich get richer the abundance will trickle down and
the poor will get richer, too. This is the "watered-down"
theory of theology, which holds that if you talk about
God's commands long enough you can usually water
them down into suggestions.

A number of people are even saying that the one
requirement is that there be no requirements. And that
would be fine if it were productive, but how many
no-requirement people are effective in job and family
and community?

Requirements may be abrasive to us, with our almost two centuries of freedom and our inheritance from the Enlightenment and the Greeks. But whether we like them or not is really irrelevant. The fact of the matter is that, if we will go *all* the way back, and not stop at the American Revolution or even at the Parthenon for that matter, we will find that our tradition is based squarely on obedience to the requirements of God.

Now a thinking man can talk about those requirements all he likes. Such talk in small groups is particularly relevant these days when we rarely articulate the requirements. But the talk had better lead to obedience rather than watering down, or a thinking man will not be faithful to his Judeo-Christian tradition. He may not *want* to be faithful, and certainly that is his privilege. But since the tradition has been around for over twenty-six hundred years and is likely to be around long after he is not, the burden of proving it an innocuous bit of whimsy is clearly upon him.

There are, the tradition says, at least these three requirements, these three rules of the game. You don't break them because experience—even without God— shows that if you do *you* will be broken. As someone has pointed out, if you jump from a tenth-story window you do not break the law of gravity, you prove the law and break yourself. Similarly the prophets in 700 B.C. were desperately trying to point out to the Jews that the more they watered down the requirements, the more vulnerable they were to corruption and defeat. Amos spoke of the requirement of justice. Hosea spoke of the requirement of love. Isaiah spoke of the requirement of humility. And Micah summarized all three.

II

"What does the Lord require of you?" he asked, "but to do justice?" Justice was first. Or more specifically, doing was first. Action, not thought. You have your orders, he was saying, now obey them. An action theology is the only one that makes sense to thinking men.

What kind of action? Justice. What does that mean? Something specific for the Jew, not vague. It meant case law.[1] What kind of case law? The kind that would restore community.[2] What kind was that? The kind that would give back justice to those from whom it had been taken. Who were such people? They could be anybody, but they were often, if not usually, poor people, widows, orphans, and those who were oppressed. "The strongly humanitarian tone and flavor of this legislation," writes a commentator about the subsequent Deuteronomic Code, "are unmistakable."[3]

It is completely beside the point to argue whether thinking men should be involved in the making of laws. According to the tradition there is no argument. It is a *requirement*. "Do justice" does not mean a vague "be nice to the people you meet on the street." The Jews were never vague, never abstract. They thought in verbs not nouns. "*Do* justice." It means do what you can to get good laws so that alienated people such as the poor and the criminal and the racially different and the elderly and the Indian and the starving and any who are oppressed may at last be restored to community. That,

---

[1] W. J. Harrelson in *The Interpreter's Dictionary of the Bible*, ed. G. A. Buttrick et al., vol. 3 (New York: Abingdon, 1962), p. 83.

[2] Ibid., p. 81.

[3] Ibid., p. 85.

astonishing as it may seem to thinking men, is the first requirement.

There is another way to restore community, and in the same breath Micah says it. "What does the Lord require of you but to do justice, and to love kindness?" Kindness is one of the great words in the Hebrew Bible. It is a noun, of course, but it was always defined by verbs. God's love meant the flight from Egypt. Man's love meant the way David loved God. It also meant, as here, the way man loved man. To love kindness meant to be obedient to one's social responsibility *beyond* law.

To illustrate: Suppose a thinking man is tutoring a potential dropout in a slum school. Certainly this is showing great kindness. But suppose at the same time he is working with the appropriate political powers to secure more tax money for desperately needy slum schools. Certainly the thinking man is far more effective if he will remember that he is required to be *both* kind *and* just.

Again, to oversimplify, but to use one of Micah's words and a word which was later used with such telling effect by Christ: love has both a social and personal dimension. The social dimension of love is justice, and the personal dimension of love is kindness. Our tradition is indebted to the Jews, primarily, for the first and to the Christians, primarily, for the second. If, however, we split the two traditions and do not hold to them both as requirements, then we become vulnerable to corruption and defeat. Love without justice is sentiment. Love without kindness can be tyranny.

The last of the three requirements in Micah's brilliant summary is humility.

> . . . What does the Lord require of you
> but to do justice, and to love kindness,
>   and to walk humbly with your God?

Humility is obviously not a "Christian" virtue. It was Jewish long before it was Christian. Originally it was an objective reference to the poor and afflicted. Later it became a subjective description of character. Its odyssey is instructive. The one thing that characterized the poor, at least objectively for the Jews, was their utter *dependence*. Whether or not they were subjectively humble—that is, poor in spirit as well as poor in income—was, of course, another matter. By the same token, what characterized the rich was their independence. Again, a rich man might have been humble and a poor man proud, but that is not the point. The point is that, for the Jews, the two major sources of pride, the opposite of humility, were wealth and power.[4] If a man had wealth and power, as many thinking men have, it was entirely possible that he would not have God. Why? Because with wealth and power you could write your own declaration of independence. And when you were independent you did not need God.

To the extent that a thinking man does justice and loves kindness, he *will* walk humbly with his God. To the extent that he walks humbly with his God, he *will* do justice and love kindness. And to the extent that he does *not* do justice and love kindness and walk humbly with his God, he *will* become vulnerable to corruption and defeat.

---

[4] Ibid., vol. 2, p. 659.

A Thinking Man

and the Resurrection

I

Nobody knows, of course, exactly what happened.
The reports are too conflicting. One says there were
several women (Luke). Another says there were two
(Mark). Another says there were a different two
(Matthew). Another says there was only one (John).

Mark and Luke say the women came to anoint the
body. Matthew that they came to see the grave.
John gives no reason why they came.

In Matthew they see an angel descending from
heaven to sit on the stone. In Mark they see a young
man in a white robe sitting in the tomb. In Luke they
see two dazzling men. In John Mary Magdalene
sees two angels inside.

We are not even sure where the appearances
occurred. Some say Jerusalem, others Galilee. Nor are
we sure how they occurred. In Matthew the women
touch the feet. In John they are expressly forbidden
to touch the feet. And in Paul, the earliest record we
have of any appearance, we are left with what must
surely be one of the most enigmatic sentences in
history: "Last of all, as to one untimely born, he
appeared also to me." But Paul tells us nothing of how
the appearance occurred. Again, we just simply do not
know exactly what happened.

II

The implications for a thinking man are lively. First, it does not really matter, does it? If it were all explained it would no longer fascinate. "Christianity is not a formula for explaining everything," Albert Schweitzer once said. "The greatest knowledge is to know we are surrounded by mystery."

Second, is it not presumptuous to expect all the answers? We do not know exactly what happened when Nero burned Rome, either, but that does not detract from our knowledge that it was burned. We do not even know, apparently, all the circumstances surrounding the death of President Kennedy, but that does not detract from our knowledge that he was killed.

Third, there would, therefore, appear to be a crucial distinction in historiography between *what* and *that*. A thinking man does not know exactly *what* happened that first Easter, but he most certainly does know *that* something happened. Since he is honest, he will be agnostic about *what* happened, but he will readily admit *that* something happened.

It is really quite useless to argue that nothing happened. We know that it did. This is not a matter for belief. It is a matter of cold historic fact. It is not a matter of going as far with your reason as you can and then taking a "leap of faith." It is a matter, simply, of reading history. We do not know exactly what happened that first Easter, but we do know that the Christian church came into being because of it. This is a fact, not an article of faith. And a thinking man does not need to be credulous or gullible to accept it.

Regardless of what happened at the tomb or in the appearances, the fact is that the disciples were turned from cowards into heroes, the extraordinary mission work of the Christian church was launched, and, to quote an anti-Christian mob in Thessalonica, the world was "turned upside down."

III

A thinking man does at least two things with the resurrection.

First, despite Schweitzer, he tries to convert the mystery into meaning. We do not like the fact that we do not know. We do not want to be agnostics. We cannot stand not knowing the details of the most important happening in history. We know the content and now we want to know the form. We know the strategy and now we want to know the tactics. Because, in other words, we know the *that*, we want to know the *what*.

The key a thinking man uses to unlock—to *try* to unlock—the mystery is metaphor. It is, unfortunately, not a very good key, but it is the best he has. The word "metaphor" comes from the Greek words meaning "to carry beyond." What we try to do with metaphors is to carry meaning from one realm of experience beyond the borders of that experience into new experience.

Thus we speak, for instance, of God as "he." It is a metaphor, and, many would argue, not a very helpful one because God, as Paul Tillich has pointed out, is "beyond personality." Nevertheless, the only way we can speak of divine experience is to speak of it in terms of human experience. That is to say, we use words from one area of life to carry us beyond that area into another.

"The ship plows the sea," is an example Webster gives. "Plow" is a metaphor because it is taken from the farm to carry us to the sea. And, to the extent that it does, it is helpful.

The trouble, of course, is that metaphors are frail vessels. They may be the best vessels we have, but their carrying power, as even that of the largest jetliner, is limited, and we begin to get into trouble. On the one hand, it is commendable for a thinking man to struggle for his metaphors. This is the audacity of the artist, and, to great or less extent, it is in all of us. On the other hand, it is naive of thinking men to think that their metaphors can do the trick. No artist would say he has caught it. No theologian would say he has caught it. No man, no matter how eloquent, would ever say he has caught the love of his wife.

The mystery is never completely unlocked by the metaphor. And whenever we think that it is, watch out. Because that is when inquisitions begin. That is when bigotry begins. When I say that my metaphor has to be your metaphor; when I say that what carries me can, will, and must also carry you; then I have violated your integrity. Metaphors are frail vessels and they will not always carry more than one at a time. That is precisely why we have so many different stories about the resurrection. John's metaphors, writing in Alexandria in A.D. 90, were not the same as Mark's writing in Rome in 65. Luke the physician's metaphors could not possibly have been the same as Paul the Pharisee's.

A thinking man is hospitable, then, to a host of metaphors. What must be done in churches is to open up every conceivable metaphor that could carry a person into the other dimension. We must have art. We must have architecture. We must have theater. We must have poetry. We must have music. Above all, perhaps, we must have music. Music just may be the language of metaphor par excellence. It may be that music is able to tell us more about the resurrection than words ever can. It "moves" us. It carries us beyond.

The church, of course, has realized this, and that is why it has always had music. But the church has never stopped there. Some people, it knows, are not "moved" by music. So the church, of all institutions, has shown hospitality to architects and artists and playwrights and poets and, believe it or not, preachers. What congregations go through as the preacher struggles to build a vessel, like Noah at work on his ark, that will carry as many of them as possible into a new experience, is nothing short of heroic.

Now the really staggering thing is that the resurrection metaphor has probably *moved* more people than any other in history. However you appropriate the metaphor that God "wins" and that his victory is proved by the experience that Christ "lives"—whether you appropriate it by music or painting or the words of the Bible or a play or a poem—however you appropriate this attempt to unlock the mystery, the fact is—and again we are in the area of fact, there can be no agnosticism here either—the fact is that that metaphor, once you are aboard, moves you not only into another dimension of life, namely the divine, it also carries you back into this dimension, the human one, on fire to do some, incredible as it may seem, divine things. "God is love," wrote the author of First John in a stunning metaphor, perhaps the most famous in the world, "and he who abides in love abides in God, and God abides in him."

In other words, the thinking man himself is the best metaphor for carrying other people into the resurrection area of experience. He lives the metaphor. That is the second thing he does with the resurrection. He shows another person not merely that something happened that first Easter but that something has happened to *him*. He is, incredible as it may seem, more apt to move back and forth between his dimension and the God dimension than he was before.

Now there are obviously many people who love and who are not Christians. And there are, obviously, many people who call themselves Christians and who do not love. But let's cut out that kind of arguing and go directly to the point. We don't want the metaphor obscuring the mystery and we don't want the arguments obscuring the meaning. The point is that the Christian is, by definition, one who loves until, if necessary, he suffers.

In our access of enthusiasm about Easter we often forget Good Friday. The one did not happen without the other. Jesus was not the Messiah they expected. He was the Suffering Servant.

It is immensely instructive that the only record we have of Jesus' resurrection appearances, aside from the one to Paul, and the one to James, is to people who already believed in him and had, to some extent, suffered with him. Maybe what the Bible is saying is that the only way a thinking man can understand the resurrection is to be moved by whatever metaphor moves him to love until he, too, suffers.

A Thinking Man

and the Trinity

Few doctrines are less understood than the Trinity.
It has confused Christian and non-Christian for
centuries. "I write about it," said St. Augustine,
"not in order to say something, but in order not to
remain silent."

Few doctrines, many say, are less in need of
understanding than the Trinity. "I sort of think it's all
irrelevant," a Christian said. "It's just a symbol anyway."

When a thinking man approaches the Trinity he is
thus confronted with two possible consequences. One
is that his thinking will carry him only so far and the
truth will be elusive. The other is that his thinking will
be stymied from the start and the truth will be irrelevant.

Nevertheless the thinking man will think. He has
spent his past week thinking about how to boost the
profits of his company, and just as he applied his brain
to *that* problem so he will be excited about applying
his brain to *this* problem.

Let us, then, ask these questions of the Trinity.
(1) What does the doctrine say? (2) Where does it
come from? (3) Can a thinking man think it?

I

The doctrine of the Trinity says that God can best be
understood by thinking of him in three ways—as Father,

Son, and Holy Spirit. That is to say, we cannot speak adequately about God without speaking about Christ and the Holy Spirit in the same breath. It is this "in the same breath" that distinguishes Christians.

The Jews have the same God. After all, Christianity sprang from Judaism. But no Jew would speak of Christ *in the same breath* that he spoke of God. Nor would a Moslem. Nor a Buddhist.

Even those religions which have a trinity would exclude Christ from it and would find the Holy Spirit, though analogous, quite impossible. The Hindus have Brahma, Siva, and Vishnu: Ultimate Reality, Destroyer, and Restorer, but no Father, Son, and Holy Spirit. The communists have Hegel's thesis, antithesis, and synthesis, but it is hardly the Christian Trinity. The Egyptians had Osiris, Isis, and Horus: Father, mother, and son. The Neoplatonists had The Good, Intelligence, and the World-Soul. Both these religions had their trinity, but neither became Christian.

It can therefore be said by a Christian scholar that

> the Trinitarian view of God has a profundity that is lacking in the abstract monotheism of Judaism and Mohammedanism. The reason is that the activity of God as Creator and Ruler of the world appears different from his activity as Redeemer of mankind in Christ and that both appear different from the indwelling Spirit which inspires the lives of those who put their trust in Him.[1]

These ideas were codified at Alexandria in the year 362 in the so-called Athanasian creed, after Athanasius, the bishop in charge of the codifying council. "We worship one God, in Trinity," says the creed, "and Trinity in Unity." "There is one Person of the Father,

---

[1] G. F. Thomas, in *The Christian Answer,* ed. H. P. Van Dusen (New York: Scribner's, 1948), p. 113.

another of the Son, and another of the Holy Ghost."
They are all one, coeternal, uncreated, incomprehensible,
and almighty. Yet there are three persons, distinguished
by the fact that the Father is unbegotten, the Son
begotten, and the Spirit proceeding from the Father
and (or through) the Son.[2]

Now a thinking man should be very clear that this
idea of God in three persons, does *not* mean that
Christians believe in three gods. They are as monotheistic
as their Jewish forebears. Nor does it mean, as a
theologian has said, that they are mathematical idiots,
saying that three persons = one person. The word
"person" translates the creed's Latin word "persona."
A persona was a mask with a megaphone mouthpiece
worn by actors in the early amphitheaters. Thus they
were able to project their voices to the thousands of
people watching the play, and, with their limited
companies, they were able to assume many roles. What
we have here, then, is one God in three roles:
Creator, Redeemer, Inspirer.

II

Where did all this come from? It came, unfortunately,
from the creed-makers. A creed is, at best, a limited
instrument. All doctrinal statements in religion share at
least these deficiencies.

One, they are late. They come long after the original
experience. There are no creeds in the Bible. There
may be laws, but there are no creeds. Nowhere can the
doctrine of the Trinity be found in the Bible. All we
have in the Bible that even suggests it are the benediction

---

[2] C. C. Richardson, *The Doctrine of the Trinity* (New York:
Abingdon, 1958), p. 13.

at the end of 2 Corinthians, the commission at the end of Matthew, and three spots where the three *personae* happen to be mentioned together.

The trinity of doctrine, it has often been pointed out, is very different from the trinity of experience. The three persons were certainly experienced by the earliest Christians, but, and this is the difference, they were never codified by the earliest Christians. They were never put into a doctrine. Later, *three hundred* years later, the doctrine came along.

A doctrine, it may be argued, is what you have to have if you do not have the experience. Often you will find that the people who are longest on doctrine are shortest on experience. This is precisely what happened in Geneva in 1553 when John Calvin and his friends burned a man named Michael Servetus because he didn't believe in their version of the Trinity.

Two, doctrine is not only late, it is conditioned. Specifically, it is conditioned by the thought-forms of the day. Some thinking men in a typical church were reading the Apostles' Creed together, and they found that they stumbled in no less than eleven places. Why? Because the thought-forms of the fourth century were obviously different from the thought-forms of the twentieth.

The failure to realize this is what makes thinking men so annoyed with the Christian church. Why must the church reverence dogmas sixteen hundred years old? Do you find science doing that to the writings of Galileo, Newton, Einstein? Of course not. Science *builds* on the writings of Galileo, Newton and Einstein. Why? Because scientists are *thinking* men, and any thinking man knows that thought-forms change and that what was true at one time is not necessarily true at another.

Why, it has been suggested, must the church be so conservative that it clutches to its bosom the bickerings of a handful of old men who had just had the illuminating Christian experience of throwing each other in jail?

It was the church that commanded Galileo, the scientist, to shut up. It was the church that was so enamored of the status quo in Germany that it allowed the Nazi juggernaut to roll over Europe. And it was the church that was so enamored of the second person of the trinity that the first slave ship to America was called the *Jesus*.

When will the church realize that the Christian gospel, "God was in Christ reconciling the world to himself," cannot be imprisoned in the thought-form of *any* day? It can be illuminated, yes, but not imprisoned. The answer is that the church will do so when it is composed of men and women who *think* about their religion as carefully as they think about their jobs. There is not a man in that typical church who would survive one week in his job if he applied to it the same tactics of commerce used in Alexandria in the year A.D. 362.

Three, doctrine is not only late and conditioned, it is almost invariably written by the wrong people. It is written by theologians when it should be written by poets. What doctrine is trying to do is describe metaphysical experience. It therefore has to use the language of meta-phor. And the language of metaphor is poetry. Or at least the artists of metaphor are the poets, not the theologians.

Poets realize that you cannot codify an experience. You cannot systematize it. You cannot put it into a resolution and have everyone vote it. That is no way to describe religious experience.

What you have to do, *all* you can do, is write what Robert Frost called "a momentary stay against confusion." It will not be adequate. It will be conditioned by the moment. It will be late. Wordsworth called it "emotion recollected in tranquillity." But it will be the best that can be done. And it will be poetry. That is why the Bible survives; creeds come and go.

III

The final question was whether, with all its deficiencies, a thinking man can think the doctrine of the Trinity. The answer would appear to be Yes *provided* the thinking man realizes the following:

One, that he is, himself, conditioned. Our own thought-forms are largely predetermined. Many people are Christians by chromosome rather than conviction. They were born into their faith and they have never really *thought* about any other. It is the same as being born American. We have never really given much thought to renouncing our citizenship.

It is thus very difficult to think objectively. Indeed it could be argued that we cannot think objectively because we are predetermined by family and country to think along certain lines. Much is made of the college rebellion and how we all try to free ourselves from the thought-forms with which we grew up. There was the recent cartoon of the college boy returning home for vacation, everyone greeting him jubilantly, and the boy greeting everyone truculently with "I don't believe in God." By the time we have our first child, however, we are often believing in God again. Objective thinking is hard.

Two, a thinking man must realize, if he would, as we say, "believe in the doctrine of the Trinity," that it is *strictly* symbolic. To the extent that its symbols reveal God for us they are true, that is, believable. To the extent that they do not reveal God they are false and unbelievable.

The language of religion is the language of symbol. The good Christian quoted at the beginning of the chapter was quite right in pointing out that the doctrine of the Trinity was a symbol. Unfortunately, however, the remark was: "It's just a symbol anyway," which reveals the subconscious disparagement of symbols which most of us make.

We would do well to remember that all language is symbolic. $E = mc^2$ is every bit as symbolic as "Father, Son, and Holy Spirit." It is standing for physical force in the universe, just as the trinitarian "formula" is standing for moral and spiritual force in the universe.

Religious language has its particular symbols just as the language of physics has its. *Neither* is "truer" than the other. Each is trying to unveil the truth *in its own way,* a fact which logical positivists and many scientists and religionists apparently find difficult to accept. How many of us know doctors, for instance, or chemists or engineers, who never go to church? By the same token, how many of us know preachers who never go to laboratories?

Religious symbols seek to unveil the truth about God. Or, "if that word [God] has not much meaning for you,"

Paul Tillich has written, "translate it, and speak of the depths of your life, of the source of your being, of your ultimate concern, of what you take seriously without any reservation."[3] When you speak of the ultimate, you have to use religious symbols. "God," says Tillich, "is the fundamental symbol for what concerns us ultimately."[4]

The important thing for a thinking man to remember is that the symbol points to a truth about God but is *not* God itself. God is more than the symbols we use to describe him. One would think this would be easy to understand, but the incomprehensible thing is that, for many Christians, it is not. Time and again the Christian symbols are literalized, that is, they are taken to *be* the reality which they *represent*. The virgin birth, for instance, is understood in biological terms, which makes it, for any thinking man, absurd. Absurdity is what happens to symbols which become what they should only represent. Or, the fall of Adam is localized in a place and person. Or, God himself is localized out there somewhere as a "he."

In this way faith turns into idolatry. To literalize is to idolize. "Thou shalt have no other gods before me," but we have made the symbol of God God. We "call something ultimate which is less than ultimate."[5] And this is what can so easily happen to the Trinity. A thinking man can turn the threefold symbol of God into God, saying this is what God is while failing to realize that there is more to God than the words we have chosen to describe him.

[3] P. Tillich, *The Shaking of the Foundations* (New York: Scribner's, 1948), p. 59.

[4] P. Tillich, *Dynamics of Faith* (New York: Harper, 1958), p. 46.

[5] Ibid., p. 52.

Three, if a thinking man would believe in the Trinity he would do well to remember that it is not only strictly symbolic, it is also *strictly* secondary. What is primary is the Bible. What is primary is to believe what a theologian who was also, surprisingly, a poet wrote in that book: "God was in Christ reconciling the world to himself." "If anyone is in Christ, he is a new creation." "To me to live is Christ."

Anything beyond that is fine, but it is *not* first. "The threefold category," writes a scholar, "may be useful, but it is not essential. We know God in a great variety of ways."[6] The scholar is right.

So if a thinking man would believe in the Trinity, he must not put God into a straitjacket. He must be wiser than his forebears. He must *think* better than they, who concluded their creed by saying, "He that will be saved *must thus* think of the Trinity."

What could be more unchristian? What, for a thinking man, could be more unthinkable?

---

[6] Richardson, *The Doctrine of the Trinity,* p. 123.

A Thinking Man's

Search for Meaning

There is an epitaph on the grave of Dag Hammarskjöld. It consists of a single word: Why?

Why? is a question the thinking man asks. It is a question that bothers him. It is a question that worries him until he dies.

Why? is a question Job asked. He was the hero of an old story about man's search for meaning. He was a paragon of the thinking man.

The unknown poet who remembered the story wrote one of the masterpieces of all time. Job, said Martin Luther, "is magnificent and sublime as no other book of Scripture."[1] "There is nothing written, I think, in the Bible or out of it," said Carlyle, "or equal literary merit."[2] "It is the greatest poem," wrote Tennyson, "of ancient and modern times."[3]

Job was a thinking man. He was also young, handsome, prosperous. He was a leader of men. He had a large family. He was known for his works of charity. He was close to God.

---

[1] Quoted by Samuel Terrien, Introduction to Job in *The Interpreter's Bible*, ed. G. A. Buttrick et al., vol. 3 (New York: Abingdon, 1954), p. 877.

[2] Ibid.

[3] Ibid.

Job, in other words, had integrity, as he reminds us in the poem. His life was of a piece. It was whole. He was at one with himself, others, and God.

But Job, the thinking man, fell upon hard times. He lost his servants. He lost his children. He lost his wealth. He lost his health. It was then that he asked the question Why? It was then that his dis-integration began.

I

One of the first things that disintegrated was Job's relationship to himself. He no longer enjoyed the peace he had once had in his original integrity. The harmony was gone, the union, the wholeness. He had become a Jekyll and Hyde, schizophrenic, not of a piece, split.

Part of Job is the old hero. He will hold fast his integrity at all costs. He will not capitulate. He will not curse God. He will not stop thinking.

But another part of Job is less attractive. He has become overweening. Maybe it was the emotional pain. Maybe the physical. Pain sometimes does that to us. It makes us turn in. And this is what Job did.

> I am innocent.
>
> I am blameless.
>
> I know that I shall be vindicated.
>
> I put on righteousness, and it clothed me.

As if that were not enough, Job even takes on God.

> I would speak to the Almighty,
>   and I desire to argue my case
>   with God. . . .
> God has put me in the wrong
>   and closed his net about me.
> Behold, I cry out. 'Violence!' but
>   I am not answered;
>   I call aloud, but there is no justice.

It is hardly different with a modern thinking man. He, too, is innocent. (Half the world goes to bed hungry.) He, too, is blameless. (Six hundred thousand people sleep in the streets of Calcutta.) He, too, knows that he shall be vindicated. (He has given his hour a week to the poor—in a jail, in a slum school.) He, too, takes on God.

Job was disintegrating so fast that at the same time he was overweening he also became, paradoxically, nihilistic. He was attracted by nothingness at the same time that he shouted his everythingness.

> I am allotted months of emptiness,
>   and nights of misery are apportioned to me.
>
> In truth I have no help in me,
>   and any resource is driven from me.

It became so bad that life itself threatened to disintegrate.

> Let the day perish wherein I was born,
>   and the night which said,
>   "A man-child is conceived."
>
> I loathe my life; I would not live for ever.
>   Let me alone, for my days are a breath.
>
> Why hast thou made me thy mark?
> Why have I become a burden to thee?
> Why dost thou not pardon my transgression
>   and take away my iniquity?

Job's Whys had led him through emptiness and sleeplessness and helplessness to the ultimate meaninglessness, to the very edge of death.

While a thinking man pursues his integrity, he is drawn to his distintegration. While he searches for God, he is searched for by death. While he desperately seeks meaning, he is hounded by meaninglessness.

II

A second thing that disintegrated was Job's relationship with other people. He was no longer at one with them as he had been, no longer at peace or of a piece, no longer integrated, no longer whole.

He had three friends. They came from a long way as friends will, each from his own home, to be with Job in his suffering. But it was not as it had been. They were split. They could not get through to him. He could not get through to them. It was the same with all his friends. They were strangers now, not friends, and in the end they took the penultimate step in disintegration between people. They ostracized him.

> They abhor me, they keep aloof
> from me;
> They do not hesitate to spit at
> the sight of me.

It is the more tragic because of his former integrity. Job, of all people, had been at one with all sorts of people.

> I delivered the poor who cried,
> and the fatherless who had none
> to help him.
> The blessing of him who was about
> to perish came upon me,
> and I caused the widow's heart
> to sing for joy. . . .
> I was eyes to the blind,
> and feet to the lame. . . .
> I broke the fangs of the unrighteous,
> and made him drop his prey from
> his teeth.
> Then I thought, "I shall die in my
> nest,
> and I shall multiply my days as
> the sand,
> my roots spread out to the waters,

with the dew all night on my
                branches,
    my glory fresh with me,
            and my bow ever new in my
                hand."

The man had done no wrong. He was a good man.
He had hoped to die in his home, with his family and
friends around him. But his children had been killed,
his friends had estranged him.

Why?

He could understand it if he had done wrong. But he
hadn't. "If I have walked with falsehood," that would
be one thing. "If my heart has been enticed to a woman,"
that would be another thing.

> If I rejected the cause of my manservant
>   or my maidservant. . . .
> If I have withheld anything that the
>   poor desired,
>   or have caused the eyes of the
>   widow to fail,
>   or have eaten my morsel alone,
>   and the fatherless has not eaten
>   of it. . . .
> If I have rejoiced at the ruin of
>   him that hated me,
>   or exulted when evil overtook him. . . .

But he hadn't. He was a good man.

Is it any wonder that he should ask for the indictment
against him? Is it any wonder that he should want to
know the charges? Is is any wonder that he should ask
the thinking man's question—Why?

III

A third thing that disintegrated was Job's relationship
with God. The original integrity was a sham. Job had
never been at one with God. If he had, he would not

have disintegrated under adversity. To be sure, he had a
relationship to the God of his fathers, of Abraham,
Isaac, and Jacob. But that was just the trouble. It was
the God of his fathers, not of Job.

The breaking up of Job's relationship to God began
in doubt. You do not ask Why if you do not doubt.
You either have the answer or, more to the point, you
trust someone who has the answer, in this case, God.
Job neither had the answer nor trusted.

Consequently he manufactured a god. He took out a
patent. God, it has been said, created man in his own
image, and man, being a gentleman, returns the
compliment. Job manufactured a god that would
vindicate him. They "carry their god in their hand,"
he said, unwittingly describing himself.

Soon, however, he moved beyond God the Idol to
God the Enemy.

> The arrows of the Almighty are
>   in me;
>   my spirit drinks their poison;
>   the terrors of God are arrayed
>   against me.

Far from being integrated with God, Job's relationship
with him disintegrated into the nadir of relationships,
war. And, as far as he is concerned, that war was started
by God. God is arbitrary, capricious, unjust. He is
immoral, tyrannical, corrupt. He is a wild beast that has
torn Job's flesh. He is a ruthless warrior who uses
him as a target.

> I was at ease, and he broke me
>   asunder;
>   he seized me by the neck and
>   dashed me to pieces;
> He set me up as his target,

> his archers surround me.
> He slashes open my kidneys, and
>   does not spare;
>   he pours out my gall on the
>   ground.
> He breaks me with breach upon
>   breach;
>   he runs upon me like a warrior.

Job fights back. It is no longer a matter of doubt but of defiance. It is no longer time for questions but for self-defense. He is Promethean in his defiance, titanic in his defense.

> I will speak.
> I desire to argue my case with God.
> I will defend my ways to his face.
> Till I die I will not put away my
>   integrity from me.

Job will not capitulate. He will not give up. He will not stop thinking. "Agree with God," says one of his friends, "and be at peace." But he cannot agree with God. He will not violate his integrity to agree with God. He will not lie for God. He will not, as a thinking man, deny the truth for God.

It is in this way that God the Enemy becomes God the Void, and Job passes through doubt and defiance to despair. "I have no hope," he says. "My hope has he pulled up like a tree."

God has gone. At least an enemy is there. But Job now knows the ultimate estrangement: he is alone in the universe. His antitheism has become atheism.

> Oh, that I knew where I might find
>   him,
>   that I might come even to his seat! . . .
> Behold, I go forward, but he is not
>   there;
>   and backward, but I cannot
>   perceive him;

> on the left hand I seek him, but I
>   cannot behold him;
> I turn to the right hand, but I
>   cannot see him.

Now there is no idol. At least Job is honest enough
not to people the void with a figment. Now there is no
enemy. There is only the awful silence of the God who
avoids him, the God who is not there.

> Oh, that I had one to hear me! . . .

"The silence of these infinite spaces frightens me,"
wrote Pascal.

He lost his servants. He lost his children. He lost his
wealth. He lost his health. Then he lost himself. He lost
his friends. He lost his God. There was nothing more
to lose. The disintegration of the thinking man
was complete.

IV

The question, of course, is, Why did it all happen?
The answer is that Job had done something most
thinking men do. He had made God unnecessary.
He could do it all on his own. His egoism, altruism,
and theism had all rendered God unnecessary.

Consider the first. Job was self-sufficient, and when
you are self-sufficient, you don't need God. Job was
autonomous, and autonomy "is practical atheism."[4]
"Job," says the Bible writer, "was righteous in his own
eyes." And when you are righteous in your own eyes,
you think you cannot be unrighteous in God's. "My
heart," said Job, "does not reproach me for any of my
days." When you're that good, God is unnecessary.
You are god.

---

[4] Samuel Terrien, *Job: Poet of Existence* (Indianapolis: Bobbs-Merrill, 1957), p. 175.

And that is how Job concludes. He uses an image of apotheosis. "Like a prince," he says, "I would approach him." In the words of William Henley's *Invictus*, which we all learned in the classic years of our egoism, adolescence: "I am the master of my fate/I am the captain of my soul." When that is true, God is unnecessary, and disintegration is entirely possible.

Consider Job's altruism. His morality, as well as his self-sufficiency, got in the way of his religion and made God unnecessary. Not only was he a great guy, he was a good one. He did all those nice things for people—visited in the jails and the nursing homes, was a father to the poor, fought for justice, and all the rest. Job was a hard man to beat for good works.

But did he do them for himself or others? It is hard to say. But one thing is certain: Job was not modest about his altruism. "I put on righteousness, and it clothed me." He used it as "a tool for self-deification."[5] When you can save yourself through your good works, you do not need God. You *are* god.

Consider Job's theism. Obviously it was a matter of god versus God. There could only be a fight. Why? Because God will brook no other gods before him.

Was God, then, the enemy or Job? Job's name, it is interesting to note, comes from the same root as the word "enemy."[6] Was God the Void, or was it Job who avoided God? Was God really silent, or was Job not listening? Was it God Job wanted to haul into court, or was it Job's conception of God?

---

[5] Ibid., p. 187.
[6] Ibid., p. 128.

V

Another question is, Did it have to happen? The answer is that it probably did. These were the necessary steps away from the unnecessary God. It was in taking them that Job demonstrated a higher integrity than he knew: he was true to what was probably the only way *he* could find God.

It is entirely possible that this is the way it has to be for a thinking man. He has to fall before he can rise. He has to go to the depths before he can rise to the heights. He has to go through egoism, of which he has plenty, to nihilism and ostracism and even atheism before he can stand in the presence of God.

Often it will take a crisis for the fall of a thinking man to begin. Occasionally, because his intellect burns with unusual imagination, a thinking man can fall without being pushed. Either way, extensive disintegration must occur if there is ever going to be integration with God, if God is ever going to be *necessary* for thinking men.

This was Job's true integrity. Not that he was righteous. Not that he was innocent. Not that he had done no wrong. But that he went all the way. *He was true to the way it had to be for him to find God.*

Then, and only then, after he had gone all the way, could grace strike. Only after he had gone through the nothingness of himself and of friendship and of ultimate meaning, could he come to the somethingness, indeed the everythingness, of God.

It may be that there is a lesson here for us all. The ways are different for different people. But only those who go all the way hear God speak. The thinking man only gets to the Yes through the Why.

Meaning's Search

for a Thinking Man

Job became a new man. The fall into disintegration was arrested, the ascent into integrity began. This was the "new being" religion talks about, and it began on the other side of God.

To get to the other side, the thinking man had to be true to the way it had to be for him to find God. He had to search for meaning before meaning could search for him. Or, if you prefer, meaning was searching for Job all along, but not until he had gone all the way with *his* search for meaning could he be found.

God speaks, in other words, but we hear *only* when we are within hearing distance. Grace comes, but *only* when we have tried to come to grace. It does not strike in the book of Job until Job has gone through thirty-seven chapters of agony in his ant-agon-ism toward God.

Grace thus is and is not gratuitous. It is there for all, for Mao Tse Tung and for Christians and Jews. But it is not effective until it has been tapped. Not until a thinking man has gone all the way, whatever his way must be, does grace strike. We have to get ourselves to the airport. The plane does not pick us up at our homes. Or, to switch the metaphor, you have to climb the mountain to get to the other side.

What happens on the other side is, of course, what fascinates. It is not at all like this side. It begins when God the Void becomes God the Voice.

I

Before, it had been Job hearing about God. Now it was Job hearing God. Before, Job had known God by hearsay. Now he knew God. Before, Job had worshiped and fought the God of his fathers. Now he was standing in the presence of the God of Job.

> Who is this that darkens counsel
>   by words without knowledge?
> Gird up your loins like a man.
>   I will question you, and you shall
>   declare to me.

The word was uranium to the Hebrews. Nothing meant more than hearing the word of God. Nothing had more value. Nothing cost as much—in terms of getting within hearing distance and in terms of obeying once the word was heard.

The major category for God's presence in the Judeo-Christian tradition is audition rather than vision. It is not what you see but what you hear. It is not how you merge with infinite light, but how you obey the infinite voice. It is not so much light in the darkness—it is the voice in the whirlwind. And even though Job says at the end "Now my eye sees thee," it is a metaphor for "Now I am within hearing distance. Now I hear. Now I will obey."

But *how* does God speak? Is it not preposterous?

Perhaps. It is entirely possible that there can be ultimate meaning for a thinking man apart from God. When a commentator speaks of "the elemental reality without which man loses the meaning of his own existence—harmony with his creator,"[1] he is right about Job, but he may be wrong about us. Have we not progressed to the point where other gods vie with God for ultimate meaning? Science? Nationalism? A thinking man's wife? His family? His company? His thinking?

The only answer is to go all the way. Try all the gods. Go the way it has to be for you. Whatever the way has to be for you, go it. But, remember, do not discard. Remember Job, a thinking man, you. He went all the way. He tried them all: egoism, altruism, theism. And when the chips were down, because he did not have God, he disintegrated. When the chips are down, which god serves you best? Put all your contenders for ultimate meaning to the test.

This is the place of art. It reminds us. Art reminds us of history—often only one man's history, as in the case of this unknown poet of Job—in such a way—emotional, volatile—that it burns into us as *our* history.

Perhaps this is why the church has for so long been a patron of the arts. If we can see, feel, touch, smell, taste how it had to be for one man, we can *imagine* how it has to be for us. And then imagination can do for thinking people what catastrophe need not. Imagination, the reading of Job, for instance, can stimulate a thinking man to be integrated with God. He need not wait for the stimulus of his child's being run over by a car.

II

God speaks. What does he say? What do his words do to Job? What happens when the Void becomes the Voice? Three things.

---

[1] Samuel Terrien, *Job: Poet of Existence* (Indianapolis: Bobbs-Merrill, 1957), p. 188.

First, he dwarfs him. He cuts Job down to size, which is precisely what one might have guessed would happen.

> Where were *you* when I laid the
>   foundation of the earth?
> Tell me, if you have understanding.
> Who determined its measurements
>   —surely *you* know!
>   Or who stretched the line upon
>   it?
> On what were its bases sunk,
>   or who laid its cornerstone? . . .

God pulls rank on Job. He steamrollers him. It is painfully evident that Job, vaunted though his intelligence may be, did not create the world, was not present at the creation of the world, does not now create what goes on in the world, and therefore has no business talking or even thinking as if he did.

It is the old idea of man's nothingness before God's everythingness, man's limitation before God's omnipotence, man's finiteness before God's infinity, man's creatureliness before God's creativity.

Just because it is old, however, does not mean it is wrong. The poet is deft. Job had heard about the omnipotence of God for years, but only now was he hearing it. The poet chose precisely what was old and made it new, made it something which, for the first time, could get through to Job's thinking machine. Why? Because Job was in *position* now to think the thought, to get the message, to hear what was being spoken to him *all along*. And, unlike the rich man in Jesus' story, he was in position well before he died.

A lot of Sunday School doesn't get through until graduate school, if then. Why? Because we are not in *position* to let it. We are not within the right distance to hear it. We have not yet gone all the way, the way it has to be for us to find God.

There is a cross on a shelf in my office carved by an eighth-grade girl at the moment she was thinking of suicide. She had gone all the way. It was then that God spoke.

Most of us, discovering new powers within ourselves throughout junior high and high school and college and beyond, build ourselves up to fight God. But

> Have *you* commanded the morning
> since your days began,
> and caused the dawn to know its
> place? . . .
> Have *you* entered into the springs
> of the sea,
> or walked in the recesses of the
> deep?
> Have *you* comprehended the
> expanse of the earth?
> Declare, if you know all this.

God dwarfs him. He puts him in his place. He puts him in perspective. Or, put it this way, God *is* whatever it is in a man's mind that reminds him he is not God.

Next, he loves him. It is not all that easy to find, but it is there. God the Voice becomes God the Father.

"Thou wilt seek me." It comes from the noun for the darkness before dawn. It is an intimation, long before God speaks, while Job is contemplating death if not suicide, that God will not let Job go, no matter how much Job lets God go.

> Thou hast granted me life and
> steadfast love;
> and thy care has preserved my
> spirit.

"Call," Job says, "and I will answer." It was the language of love.

> Thou wouldest call, and I would
>   answer thee;
>   thou wouldest long for the work
>   of thy hands.
> For then thou wouldest number
>   my steps,
>   thou wouldest not keep watch
>   over my sin.

He is talking about how it would be after death. He is asking that God remember him in the ultimate somethingness of life beyond the nothingness of death.

It is only a glimmer, of course, only an intimation.

> The mountain falls and crumbles
>   away [Job says at once],
>   and the rock is removed from its
>   place;
> the waters wear away the stones;
>   the torrents wash away the soil
>   of the earth;
>   so thou destroyest the hope of
>   man.

But on the other side of God we can only infer the love that was adumbrated on this side.

The very fact, for instance, that God would speak at all implies his love. Especially in view of Job's slander. The speaking proves that God is not a stranger. Strangers do not speak.

The fact, too, that God did not accuse Job, did not haul him into court, did not indict him, implies love. It is extraordinary, but God never directly chastises Job for his monstrous egoism. He never takes him to task for his self-centered altruism. And he never reproves him for his atheism.

Is this the way it is with God and thinking men?
Is the incredible forgiveness always there? Is it true, as
Tillich says, that all we have to do is accept the fact
that we are accepted? In spite of everything, we are
forgiven? Is this the Good News?

Again, there is the merest sketch of proof. The greatest
love that can be shown is the willingness of someone
to suffer with and even for another. In Job, God begins
to suffer. He is not ready to go all the way. But he begins,
in a rudimentary way, to be more involved, perhaps,
than he was before. God the Father becomes, in only a
hint, God the Son.

The unknown poet's thinking was so imaginative that
he speaks on various occasions of a redeemer, an
umpire, an advocate, a witness, an intercessory angel.

> If there be for him an angel,
>   a mediator, one of the thousand,
>   to declare to man what is right
>   for him; . . .
> Then man prays to God, and he
>   accepts him. . . .

It is the mediator, perhaps, the one who suffers with us
and for us, who brings a thinking man within hearing
distance of God, and God within speaking distance
of a thinking man.

Lastly, God mystifies Job. When God speaks, what he
does not say is as important as what he says. He does not
give the thinking man answers. He does not solve the
problem of evil or the riddle of injustice. He does not
publicly vindicate Job.

Why? Again it is a matter of perspective. If we knew
the answers then we would be gods. It is the fruit of the

tree of *knowledge* that, paradoxically, *thinking* men must *not* eat. Ultimate questions are hidden in ultimate mystery. "Christianity," we heard Schweitzer saying, "is not a formula for explaining everything. The greatest knowledge is to know we are surrounded by mystery."

This has some corollaries. *One* is that we should be patient, and this, perhaps is the hardest of all virtues for the thinking man. The very word comes from the root for "suffer." The patience of Job was that he fought through, impatiently, to the point where, on the other side of God, he could be patient—that is, to the point where, as a thinking man, he could stand to live without answers.

> The greatest happiness of the thinking man [said Goethe] is to fathom what can be fathomed and quietly to reverence what is unfathomable.

Another corollary is that we must, therefore, beware of a too-quick orthodoxy. Orthodoxy is prone to release us from thinking. It is eager to supply answers where there are no answers. It is happy to be reductionist where it should be expansionist, inflexible where it should be protean.

Ultimate meaning cannot be reduced to a few propositions. Psychology cannot be reduced to the first six months of life. Economics cannot be reduced to the way a thinking man runs his firm.

This is where Job's three friends went askew. They were classically orthodox, thinking they could reduce ultimate mystery into ultimate meaning. It is they, then, rather than Job, who abandon the struggle as thinking men, are ultimately *impatient,* and who, strange to say, perhaps because their minds are logic-chopping engines, show no mercy, no kindness, no love. Job, then, is a better man as an atheist than they are as theists.

Ethical monotheism when it provides a method for spelling out rationally the mystery of God, is utterly separated from the reality which it seeks to interpret. It negates God by the very fact that it claims to comprehend him. It creates an idol in the image of man's mind. The monotheism of the friends has become the mere projection of their idea of justice.[2]

A *final* corollary, then, is that the heretic just may be closer to God than the too-quickly orthodox. Why? Because the heretic, in despairing of final answers, is in a better position to throw himself on the mercy of God.

We are justified when we are mystified. When a thinking man says he *does not know* but trusts God, then he is at last close to God. His distance is being overcome. You can handle the mystery, in other words, if you've got the trust. And you can get the trust if you go all the way, the way it has to be for you to find God.

The function of an orthodoxy which has died is to spur heretics to lose hope in all human props, until they are prepared to receive grace alone.[3]

Existence is fulfilled when man is aware, not of his ultimate concern but of becoming the concern of the ultimate.[4]

We do not see the answer; we trust the Answerer. . . . We do not gain the victory; we are united with the Victor.[5]

Job is not vindicated, or even answered, but loved. That is meaning's search for the thinking man.

---

[2] Ibid., p. 69.
[3] Ibid., p. 100.
[4] Ibid., p. 239.
[5] Ibid., p. 197.

A Thinking Man

on the Other Side of God

Job fights God. God speaks. Job is changed. It is the
thesis-antithesis-synthesis of the religious life. Is is the
dialectical idealism of a thinking man's faith.

Job had disintegrated in crisis. God spoke. Job,
on the other side of God, is integrated with God,
others, himself.

I

The extraordinary thing is that Job should have been
integrated at all. It is not so much what God said as
how he said it. It is not only that he questioned rather
than answered Job, it is that his questions dripped
with irony.

> Have *you* commanded the morning
>   since your days began,
>   and caused the dawn to know its
>   place? . . .
> Have *you* entered into the springs
>   of the sea,
>   or walked in the recesses of the
>   deep? . . .
> Have *you* comprehended the expanse
>   of the earth?
> Declare, if you know all this.

But Job cannot declare. And God knows that he
cannot. Nevertheless he piles irony on irony, for he
has an end in mind.

Can *you* bind the chains of the
        Pleiades,
    or loose the cords of Orion?
Can *you* lead forth the Mazzaroth
        in their season,
    or can *you* guide the Bear with
        its children? . . .

Do *you* give the horse his might?
    Do *you* clothe his neck with
        strength?
Do *you* make him leap like the
    locust? . . .

Is it by *your* wisdom that the hawk
        soars,
    and spreads his wings toward the
        south?

Is it at *your* command that the
        eagle mounts up
    and makes his nest on high? . . .

Shall a faultfinder contend with
        the Almighty?
    He who argues with God, let
        him answer it.

But Job cannot.

    I lay my hand on my mouth.
I have spoken once, and I will not
        answer;
    twice, but I will proceed no
        further.

The first thing that happens to a thinking man on the
other side of God is that he is silent. Job, who had
shaken his fist at God; Job, who would plead his case
before God; Job, who would defend himself to the
death before God, is silent. It is the first step, after God
speaks, in a thinking man's integrity. The descent into

disintegration is arrested and the ascent into integrity begins when a thinking man lays his hand on his mouth.

The ironic method beats a man into silence. For the first time a thinking man sees himself in perspective. No longer is he mesmerized by his thinking machine. No longer does he adulate himself. "Like a prince I would approach him." But no longer does he fight God as a god.

The world of nature, who is a thinking man before it? The open spaces, the national parks, the lakes, the wild animals, who is a thinking man before them? Before the demands of his job, his home, of peace?

Job, who thought he had climbed so high, had fallen so low. Job, whose thinking was so creative that he thought he was another Creator, was only a creature. He cannot answer the ultimate questions. He is silent. He cannot rule in the place of God. And God makes sure that he knows it with final irony.

> Have you an arm like God,
>   and can you thunder with a voice
>   like his?
> Deck yourself with majesty and
>   dignity;
>   clothe yourself with glory and
>   splendor.
> Pour forth the overflowings of your
>   anger,
>   and look on every one that is
>   proud, and abase him. . . .
> Then will I also acknowledge to
>   you,
>   that your own right hand can give
>   you victory.

But there will be no acknowledgement. Job's own right hand cannot give him victory over himself. He cannot, on his own, abase himself. He needs God. Without God, he will be vociferous about Job. With

God, he will be silent. God *is* whatever it is that makes a thinking man keep quiet.

II

Second, a thinking man on the other side of God believes. Note the position. The faith comes *after* the grace. It is on the other side of God, not on this side. What is on this side is man's search for God, a first step in faith but not complete faith. Not until man has experienced God's search for him is there faith. "Faith," Luther said, "is our *response* to God's grace."

Job responds.

> I know that thou canst do all
> things,
> and that no purpose of thine can
> be thwarted.

Now he is no longer the searcher but the searched. He is no longer the questioner but the questioned. He is no longer the seeker but the sought. When he knows this, and responds to it, that is faith.

There are two stages of faith: doubt before belief, atheism before theism, war before peace, search before response. *Both* stages are necessary in a thinking man's search for meaning. Both are necessary in meaning's search for a thinking man.

On this side of God, we may know about grace but we do not respond to it. We may have read about it but we have not experienced it. We may have been told about it but we have not been struck by it.

III

Third, Job confessed. Note the order. This is exactly the way it is in the book. The poet knew the way it had to be for a thinking man: silence, faith, confession.

Confession was, of course, the opposite of assertion, the opposite of pride. It is a complete about-face for Job. It is even more startling when you read what he said. He was short and to the point. "I despise myself," he said. A thinking man cannot change his thinking about himself any more than that.

It is not something you can say on this side of God. On this side of God we are princes. On this side of God we are gods. Only on the other side of God do we despise ourselves.

It is strong language. The word comes from the root to "melt," "dissolve," "sink." It is, in a sense, Job's ultimate disintegration. His ego is melted away. The dissolution of the old Job is complete. He has sunk out of sight.

And that, the poet is saying, is the way it has to be for a thinking man and God. For God to take over a thinking man has to go under. He has to drown. "He who would lose his life," a later thinking man said, "will find it."

On this side of God it is impossible. On the other side of God it is inevitable. On this side of God it makes no sense. On the other side of God there is no other sense. On this side of God a thinking man will fight if you tell him he has to dissolve. On the other side of God a thinking man will tell you he is, at last, at peace.

For the first time Job is able to say the last thing a thinking man, on this side of God, would say. He makes the ultimate confession for a thinking man.

> I have uttered what I
>   did not understand,
>   things too wonderful for me,
>   which I did not know.

The ultimate confession for a thinking man is to say that he does not know. The old Job is dead. The new Job is being born. "This my son was dead, and is alive again; he was lost, and is found."

IV

Fourth, a thinking man on the other side of God repents. Note again the position. The repentance comes *after* the grace. It, too, is on the *other* side of God, not on this side. You cannot repent your way to God. You repent your way *from* God. Repentance is not something you do to stand in the presence of God. It is something you do because you have stood in the presence of God.

There is not, in other words, a series of steps you take to find God. You do not listen, believe, confess, repent and all the rest to find God. You do these things *because* you have *been* found by God.

On this side of God it is *impossible* to do these things. We will shout, fight, assert, defy. But "with God," as the later thinking man said, "all things are possible." And on the *other* side of God, it is *inevitable* that we listen, believe, confess, repent, and all the rest.

The *one* thing that has to be done on this side of God is to go all the way, to be true to the way it has to be for us, as thinking men, to find God. Which means we have to be true to the way it has to be for us to disintegrate, dissolve, melt.

"I . . . repent," Job said. In the New Testament sense, as we have seen, it was to come to mean that he had "changed his mind" about his behavior. The thinking man's about-face was complete. It was even so complete that he could use the ironic method against himself:

> "Who is this that hides counsel
>   without knowledge?" [he quotes God] . . .
> "Hear, and I will speak;
>   I will question you, and you declare to me."

When a man can be ironic with himself, when he has a sense of humor about himself, it is one of the first signs that his distances are being overcome.

V

Fifth, a thinking man on the other side of God atones. After he has gotten himself in perspective, he is in position to atone for being out of perspective. First the distance between himself and God is overcome by listening and believing. Then the distance within himself is overcome by confessing and repenting. Then a thinking man is in position to have the distance between himself and other people overcome by atoning, by making up for the wrongs he has done them, or, curiously, that *they* have done *him*.

The word atone, as we have seen, means to be at one. It is the same meaning as integrity, which means whole. On this side of God Job had disintegrated. On the other side of God he was integrated, or at one, with God, himself, and other people.

It is almost unthinkable what Job, on the other side of God, does to his friends who had bullied him with their orthodoxy. He prays for them. He asks God to forgive them. "Father, forgive them" the later thinking man was to say. And Job does in the story what Jesus did in history.

Again, this is not the kind of thing we can do on this side of God. If someone wrongs us and we are split from him rather than at one, we want to get back at him. We do not want to forgive him. We would rather be a stranger to him than a friend.

Good works *follow* grace, they do not precede it. A thinking man cannot work his way to God. When he is at one with God, then he will be at one with himself, and then he will be at one with others. His going out to them in suffering love, love that forgives and does not count the cost, will be inevitable. But on this side of God, that kind of love is anything but inevitable. It is often a self-centered morality, Job's morality, the kind which does good for others because it makes the self feel good.

Does this mean that there is no morality on this side of God? No. What it means is that good works on this side of God are voluntary and suspect; on the other side of God they are involuntary and good. There are, then, or should be, no such thing as "volunteers" in churches. They are "involuntaries," the thinking men and women on the other side of God, who are at one with others because God is at one with them. Racial "integration" we used to say. It is one proof of a thinking man's integrity.

VI

Sixth, a thinking man on the other side of God enjoys good fortune. He prospers. It is a Hollywood ending for Job, and some scholars have been so astonished that they have said it was added by a later hand than the unknown poet's.

Job gets twice as much property as he lost. He has seven sons and three exceptionally beautiful daughters. And he sees his grandchildren to the fourth generation.

It may be fabulous. It may have been added. But even if it is both, there is a meaning behind the mystery behind the words. And the meaning is this. On the other side of God, no matter what a man's circumstances, he prospers. When we are at one with God, good fortune is ours, inevitably. We may not own twice as much or have twice

as large a family or live twice as long, but good fortune
is ours, we prosper.

"I have learned," Paul wrote from jail, "in whatever
state I am, to be content." "I count it all joy, my
brethren, when I meet various trials." "I have the feeling,"
said a woman in a small group explaining God's grace in
her life, after a terrible crisis, "I have the feeling that
nothing could shake me."

VII

Last, a thinking man on the other side of God gets his
mind's delight. He is wise. It is the wisdom which comes
from retrospect. It is the wisdom which comes on the
other side of God.

Now Job knew what integrity meant. Now he knew
what suffering meant. Now he knew what Job meant.

He did not have all the answers, to be sure.
But now he had God, and that meant he could live
with the questions.

"The Almighty—we cannot find him," his fourth friend,
the good one, had said. But Job did not know that on
this side of God. Now, on the other side of God, he knew.

"I have uttered what I did not understand." But Job
did not know that on this side of God. Now, on the
other side of God, he knew.

What a thinking man knows on the other side of God,
he does not know on this side. Indeed, he cannot. He has
to stand in awe before himself before he can kneel in
silence before God.

This is a thinking man's integrity: that, at all costs,
whatever the price in suffering, he will be true to the way
it has to be for him to find God. Then, and only then,
can he be found.